INTUITIVE PSYCHOTHERAPY

INTUITIVE PSYCHOTHERAPY
The Role of Creative Therapeutic Intervention

William N. Confer, Ph.D.
Clinical Director

Wiregrass-Comprehensive Mental Health System
Dothan, Alabama

 HUMAN SCIENCES PRESS, INC.
72 FIFTH AVENUE
NEW YORK, N.Y. 10011-8004

To my greatest inspirations:
My wife, Karin, and my children, Ryan and Kristen

Printed in the United States of America
987654321

Library of Congress Cataloging-in-Publication Data

Confer, William N.
  Intuitive psychotherapy.

  Bibliography: p.
  Includes index.
  1. Psychotherapy.   2. Intuition (Psychology)
3. Creative ability.   4. Imagination.   I. Title.
[DNLM: 1. Creativeness.   2. Problem Solving.
3. Psychotherapy—methods.   WM 420 C748i]
  RC480.5.C5776   1987   616.89'14   86-27506
  ISBN 0-89885-337-0

CONTENTS

8   INTUITIVE PSYCHOTHERAPY

ACKNOWLEDGEMENTS

To Steve Young and Glen King for their ideas, to Karin Confer and Charles McArthur for their support, to Joan Burns and Glen Bannister for their time and suggestions, and to my clients for teaching me—I most respectfully thank you all.

INTRODUCTION AND OVERVIEW

Knowledge is Power.

—Thomas Hobbs

Imagination is more powerful even than knowledge.

—Albert Einstein

As a psychotherapist, I have observed that many clients tend to apply inefficient and ineffective strategies to solve everyday problems in dealing with self and others. This tendency does not appear tied to any particular dilemma or set of predisposing factors that contribute to the formation of an individual's problems in living. However, the flawed conceptualizations from which the faulty problem-solving strategies are derived certainly predispose the individual to continuing problems in living. In short, problems in living in many cases appear to be synonymous with uncreative problem-solving strategies. Because the strategies employed are untenable, problem situations recur and "tried, but untrue" approaches are reapplied. As a psychotherapy supervisor, I have occasionally noticed on my own part and that of many otherwise competent therapists the tendency to replicate this process from the other side of the relationship. Marginally effective psychotherapeutic interventions may be persistently reapplied while other highly effective alternatives are overlooked. By overcoming conceptual blocks to problem understanding and by applying more influential problem-solving strategies, impasses can be overcome and presenting issues resolved. One intention of this book is to offer the reader a variety of effective ways to free oneself and clients from conceptual stagnation. Specific strategies are described not only to escape stereotypic or self-limiting thinking, but also to tap the wisdom of one's creative imagination.

The success of a therapeutic intervention is not based solely upon its internal merits, but also upon the way it is structured and presented to the client. A useful intervention can be made more potent by fine-tuning it to a particular client's sensitivities and inclinations. Therefore, the subject of this book is not just how to free the resources of the creative imagination in the service of psychotherapy. It is also how to apply these newly aroused resources to powerful means of influencing the thoughts and actions of those in treatment. Interventions that evolve from this raw material correspond to those of some of the most innovative therapists to date. Others share an affinity with the tactics of compliance experts in our culture: advertisers, salespersons, lobbyists, fund raisers, politicians, and bunco artists. All are liberally illustrated in the text with case examples.

A playful examination of blocks to creative thinking and problem solving in client and therapist alike serves as a springboard to specific therapeutic interventions that enliven any therapeutic approach, whether predominently behavioral, cognitive, emotive, or dynamic in emphasis. Because the intention of this book is to infuse creativity into the process of any therapy rather than to prescribe what is examined in therapy, examples and formats are provided from which the reader can combine his unique talents to create a therapeutic approach that is more integrated, far-reaching, spontaneous, and freer from distorted assumptions than before.

My interest and intention is to bring the fun and the wonder inherent in any creative endeavor to the practicing psychotherapist who wants to polish his therapy skills and help others live more creative lives. The reader who opens himself to this book will not only become more intuitive and influential; he will also become more trusting of his intuition and the creative problem-solving strategies that follow.

Note: The convention of using "client" in the singular has been retained except in illustrations with couples or families. This is not to imply that the methods and strategies are limited to individual therapy in these cases.

The convention of using masculine gender for statements that apply to both sexes has been retained to avoid clumsy construction. No sexism is intended. In fact, the author believes sexual bias works against the attainment of accurate intuition.

Names and other identifiable characteristics have been changed throughout the text to ensure the privacy of clients.

CHAPTER 1

CONCEPTUAL ORGANIZATION
OF EXPERIENCE

The map is not the territory.

—S. I. Hayakawa

When Roger Bannister was a child he severely burned his legs in a school accident. He was told by his physician that he would never walk again. As an adult he became the first person to break the 4-minute mile.

Most individuals have heard a true-life tale of a woman who ordinarily cannot carry two 20-pound bags of groceries and yet is able to pick up the front end of a car in order to save the life of her child. In a similar vein is the action of a war hero who behaves courageously in the face of the enemy; only afterwards does he look back in astonishment at his performance.

Warts are the result of a virus that makes cells multiply. The body's immune system has frequently proven itself to be ineffective in combatting the invasion of the virus. Under hypnosis, however, many individuals have been able to remove warts through accepting the suggestion of a hypnotist that the touch of a pencil tip will lead to their disappearance.

The track star, the loving mother, the war hero, and the wart sufferer all share a commonality: all stepped outside the conventional conceptualization of what is possible and, by doing so, reached a new level of potential that may be described as "miraculous." Roger Bannister rejected the "proper" understanding of his limitations. The mother and the war hero, each geared to the necessity of the moment, temporarily suspended their understanding of their capabilities. The wart sufferer, having little or no conceptualization of the cause or cure of warts, became receptive to one offered by the hypnotist.

These four cases, while extreme, demonstrate a very important characteristic of conceptualization: While conceptions of what is possible help organize experience and free an individual from examining irrelevant or unlikely possibilities, these same conceptualizations also limit one's acceptance and understanding of inner potential. This feature of concepts holds both for those that have a basis in fact (such as scientific theory) or a basis only in faith (such as voodoo, superstitions, and placebo effects). Nearly all concepts, of course, are combinations of fact and fancy, evidence and lore. Consider the frequent observation by psychotherapists of two individuals who may be quite similar in symptoms and circumstances, but vary greatly in degree of handicap. The difference between the two is one of conceptualization of problems or capacities or both.

Clients frequently possess self-limiting conceptualizations that therapy seeks to expand to more realistic proportions. The actualization of client's potential through therapy may differ in degree from the extraordinary accounts given above, but varies little in form. Consider the example of a male client who steadfastly believes himself to be shy. Perhaps he consciously reviews prior interactions selectively for shyness and tells himself he has no alternative to inferiority and inadequacy in the presence of strangers. At the same time this person is as capable as anyone else of making social gestures, learning interesting conversation gambits, and using the English already within his repertoire to become articulate in the context of strangers. With the possible exceptions of extreme mental retardation or physical limitations, this person could be as outgoing as anyone else were he not confined unnecessarily by beliefs of what is possible. In fact, if he is asked during a group therapy session to pretend to be the outgoing person he is not, he actually becomes one temporarily.

This book will explore ways to help clients remove obstacles that maintain limiting conceptualizations as well as means to tap fully one's potential as a creative therapist. Before these topics are discussed in the following chapters, it will be helpful to examine the process of conceptualization in more detail.

FROM INNATE ORGANIZING TENDENCIES TO MODELS OF THE WORLD

Please examine Figure 1.1 for a moment. What do you see? Notice how you automatically perceive it as a circle made of dots rather than a set of randomly distributed dots on a page. The fact is, one cannot help but conceptualize; human beings are organizing animals. Give an individual an ambiguous stimulus and he will organize and interpret it in some manner to find meaning. Rollo May (1975) described this organizing tendency within individuals as an "innate striving toward meaning" (p. 14).

One's organized ideas about "the way the world works" are called by many names by a variety of theoreticians and practitioners. Alfred Adler coined the term "life-style" to denote an individual's cognitive organization. It became his concept for the convictions one develops early in life to organize current experience and from which to base predictions for future experience (Mosak & Dreikurs, 1973, pp. 39-40). Piaget describes one's personal theory about the world as "schema." New data are assimilated into existing schema and the schema itself is modified by experience so that the map closely resembles the world it emulates. The innovators of a cognitive therapy for depression (see Beck, Rush, Shaw, & Emery, 1979), have also chosen schemas to represent enduring cognitive patterns that have developed from an individual's interactions with the environment. For this group, schemas are defined as "abstract and generalizable rules regarding regularities in relationships among internal represen-

Figure 1.1.   Do you see randomly distributed dots or a circle made of dots?

tation of events" (Rush & Giles, 1982, p. 163). Schemas are generated for particular sets of events; the matrix of all schemas de-
vised by an individual corresponds closely to a worldview.

The learning theorist, E. C. Tolman (1959), used the term
"cognitive map" to denote an expectation for a particular set
of circumstances, much in the same way Beck uses the term
schema. For one's larger expectation that the world is organized
in certain ways he reserved the term "sign-gestalt-expectation."
The Transactional Analysis originator, Berne (1961), dubbed

sign-gestalt-expectations "life scripts." Still others describe them as "world images" (Watzlawick, 1978, ch. 5) and "models of the world" (Bandler & Grinder, 1975, part one). These collections of ideas may not be as rigorous as scientific exploration and are only partially conscious; however, they are thought to be fully operative. They are more or less accurate. Like road maps to which the concept is compared, these cognitive maps appear to simplify some experiences and summarize others in order to maximize the limited faculties of people and to minimize confusion. Selective elements thought to be more relevant stand out in sharp relief; other detail is either distorted or omitted altogether.

Where do the ideas that compose worldviews come from? Why do some ideas just pop up, while others require much deliberate effort? The origin of the word *idea* gives a clue. It is derived from the Greek *ideim*, which means "to see." All ideas begin with the senses and from there proceed through a number of channels and modifications to find their place within or to transform one's world view. All through this process the "wired in" tendency to organize and optimize stimuli appears to operate at the peripheral nervous system level and continues at the central nervous system level.

Sensory endings react to changes in stimuli which are collected and organized at the sensory level and then transmitted to the brain. At this central nervous system level the messages are interpreted according to the laws of perception.

Traces of experiences are stored in the brain for later retrieval. Experience is further organized at the storage level to maximize an individual's limited capacity to receive, process, and remember data. Landmark research by Miller (1956) persuasively demonstrates the ability to manipulate seven plus or minus two "chunks" of information at any given time. By organizing vast amounts of data into sequences of manageable chunks, an individual can elasticize his limited span of attention and memory capacity. For example, suppose a person wanted to remember the following sequence of 24 numbers: 106614921776181218651945. The task is greatly facilitated by organizing them into six sets of important dates in Anglo-American history (i.e., 1066, 1492, 1776, and so on.) Perhaps this chunking capacity has something to do with the choice of seven plus or minus two units in phone numbers, zip codes, days of the week, notes on the musical scale, and so on.

One's normal sensory, perceptual, and contextual (conceptual) processes provide optimal functioning (given our limited resources) to go about the business of being in the world. The brain can only process so much; therefore, the most important stimuli get through. Rough edges and incongruities are chipped away to provide maximal storage and recall as well as physiological and psychological homeostasis.

Some organized experiences become symbolized into language for easier reflection (i.e., talking to oneself) and communication to others. Language is a means to represent organized experience through agreed upon sounds and squiggles. These sounds and squiggles enable an individual to create abstractions by using sensory experience metaphorically. In doing so, the range of expression is extended dramatically. Bandler and Grinder (1975) label the sensory metaphors through which organized experience is communicated as "representational systems." Consider the abstraction "I understand" from their book to illustrate this. It can be expressed in the language of vision ("I see"), audition ("I hear you"), gustation ("That leaves me with a good taste in my mouth"), kinesthetics ("I grasp your meaning") and, perhaps, in terms of other sensory channels as well. Even the word "understand" is thought to derive from the visual image of standing under a posted set of laws that was to be obeyed (Jaynes, 1976, p. 199). Olfaction appears to be less relied upon than other senses by humans. This likely accounts for the relative paucity of olfactory expressions in language.

The abstraction process of language lends even greater flexibility to one's organizing tendency. With language one can organize not only by sensation, but also by symbols for sensation. By abstracting commonalities and ignoring differences, everything can become a metaphor for everything else. Individuals can be "pressured" into activities or become a "brighter" person and do what "sounds" right in order to avoid "bitter" consequences or otherwise become "stuck." As experience is symbolized for communication and storage purposes, more flexibility is available to conceptualize issues that face the individual. This great flexibility afforded in encoding experience leaves a lot of room for individuals to be creative in recombining stored experiences and in integrating new ones. The other side of the coin, however, is that there is also much room for ambiguity and erroneous combinations.

SOURCES OF MISCONCEPTION IN WORLD MODELS

There is a trade-off in the conceptualization process. The sensory, perceptual, retentional, and linguistic processes that give economy of organization and flexibility are the very ones that all but guarantee the likelihood of forming a number of misconceptions.

Sense receptors are sensitive to only a small range of possible stimuli, thus omitting all others of that class that could help in discrimination. The receptors of visual stimuli, for example, react to only the smallest portion of the electromagnetic spectrum (400-700 billionths of a meter within a spectrum range of less than one billionth to a thousand meters). Ultraviolet light is undetected by human visual receptors. Other wavelengths are actually heard or felt rather than seen. Even within these visible wavelengths individuals are sensitive to only a small window of visual stimuli. Ordinary pond water seen with the eyes is transformed under the microscope to a world teaming with microorganisms. What is true for vision is true for the other sensory channels as well. In addition, human beings are wired to react only to changes and contrasts in this limited range of stimuli. If stimuli do not vary, nerve endings habituate and cease firing. The limited reception on this fundamental level is subject to central nervous system pruning at higher levels.

All perception (organized and interpreted sensory data) is selective, and necessarily so. Individuals become overwhelmed (hyperactive) unless they attend to what appear to be relevant stimuli and prune what appear to be irrelevant from the constant bombardment of stimuli assaulting all the senses. Akin to phenomena at the sensory level, individuals stop recording oversaturated input at the perceptual level. For example, take a look at the back of your hand. Really look at it. Notice the texture of the skin, the hairs, and curls of skin and vessels. How well did you know the back of your hand?

Perceptual selective attention is further colored by temporary states of deprivation and heightened emotion and all manner of prior learning. Current perception is compared to expectations and incompatibility tends to be dealt with by modifying one or the other through deletion, distortion, or generalization. Bruner and Postman (1949) offer a classic study of deletion of incongruency in the perceptual process. Subjects were briefly exposed to playing cards and asked to identify each one. Most of the cards were identical to typical playing cards, but a few had red spades or black hearts. Even on short exposures, most cards were identified correctly by subjects. The anomalous cards were also identified without hesitation as either red hearts or black spades. The incongruencies were simply erased. As exposure time increased, some subjects modified their conceptions to account for the discrepant cards and accurately identified them; other subjects became acutely distressed. Even at 40 times the average exposure necessary to accurately identify normal cards, over 10 percent of the anomalous ones were never identified correctly.

Incongruous input that is not deleted may become distorted to fit one's current model of the world. The "love is blind" phenomenon is such a case. Finally, overly inclusive generalizations may occur. Here is an innocent example common to young children: "This rabbit is white and furry; therefore, all white and furry animals are rabbits." A more pernicious example in adulthood at a conceptual level may be something like: "I was hurt by this woman whom I trusted not to hurt me; therefore, I can trust no woman and all women hurt." Organization of experience at the perceptual level influences conceptions, and conceptions can reciprocally influence interpretations of sensory stimuli. A brief review of how prior experience is thought to be stored and conceptualized follows.

Try the following exercise in memory as reported by Jaynes (1976, p. 29) in his fascinating study of consciousness. Remember the last time you were at the beach. Take as much time as you need to capture this image vividly before reading on. What do you see? Most people see themselves either lying in the sand or frolicking in the surf as though watching a movie. However, this was never the experience at all. Unless individuals had a mirror in front of them, they never experienced *seeing* themselves at the beach even though that is the way it is recalled. Memory is not a passive recording of experience at all; memory is productive.

Forgetting is the other side of the coin to memory. New experience is thought to impede and distort recollection of stored material (retroactive interference) and old material is thought to impair retention of more freshly learned phenomena (proactive interference). Consider the example of Professor Smith who deals with new students occupying seats of students from the prior term. She may have a tendency to call the new student by the name of the former occupant (proactive interference), or she may have difficulty recalling the name of the previous occupant as she comes to know the current occupant (retroactive interference).

(By the way, were you surprised to discover Professor Smith to be female? Given the abstraction of "professor" many have a tendency to interpret it according to a model of the world where the "best guess" is male.)

As likely as individuals are to arrive at erroneous conceptualizations as a result of information-processing mechanisms, the condition can be further compounded by the imperfection of language for the communication of ideas and experiences. Imperfect conceptualizations are transmitted by imprecise symbols that are variably interpreted by the receiver according to his own conceptualizations. When experiences are recoded linguistically, some of the particulars of the experience can become diluted as the level of abstraction rises. For example, one could start with the rather concretized expression of "Bill Confer." One level up the abstraction ladder might be "man." This could be followed by "human being," then "earthling," and proceed all the way up to "carbonized matter." If it is agreed that each of these true statements loses something in the abstraction process, imagine what happens to individuals as they attempt to communicate such difficult abstractions as love, truth, justice, and so on. Yet, issues of trust, love, and dignity are common among those seeking psychotherapy and cry out for a common understanding between client and others. As probable as faulty conceptualization is, the communication of faulty conceptualization can make the message even more obscure.

Individuals assign what are believed to be the essential attributes of a class. All appear to develop subliminal rules about how a particular class relates to other classes, what can and cannot be done within and between classes, and how classes can be restructured. Most of the chaff, but also some of the grain, is lost in the harvesting of all that is to be integrated, organized, and synthesized. A simple example of this is the universal one of the first impression. The concept of a stranger is based upon all past and present organized experience and is frequently quite accurate. Occasionally, the first impression can stray far from the mark.

Much of an individual's worldview is comprised of information from indirect sources rather than from direct experience. Albrecht (1980, pp. 121-122) estimates that only about one-eighth of what any person knows is the product of direct experience. The lion's share of one's model of the world is from assumptions and inferences about the unknown or novel made on the basis of what has been experienced or from descriptions, reports, judgments, inferences, and assumptions reported to the individual by others. Information is accepted from a variety of sources with varying degrees of critical appraisal. Using your formal education as an example, how much did you learn from actual experience with the subject (e.g., laboratory classes) and how much learned material was from taking in material of which the validity was simply accepted (e.g., lecture classes)?

Even direct experience is no guarantee of correct conceptualization because each new "fact" is placed in the context of other conceptions which comprise one's model of the world. The context modifies the meaning of the fact. The famous Müller-Lyer illusion illustrates this analogically (Figure 1.2). Both lines are identical in length, yet one is interpreted as shorter than the other because of its placement in the context of the other lines. Similarly, $100 can mean a great deal to a poor person, but mean little to a wealthy one. As a final example, take pause for a moment and describe to yourself a zebra. Most Americans describe a zebra as a horselike animal that is white

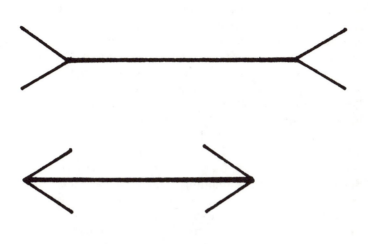

Figure 1.2.   The Müller-Lyer illusion.

with black stripes. In Africa, where most people are black-skinned, the population would agree that a zebra is horselike, but report it to be a black animal with white stripes (Berlitz, 1982, p. 143).

Misconceived models of the world appear to be inevitable outcomes. The very internal strategies individuals possess to optimize their limited resources necessarily create a source of error in order to minimize additional sources of error. Individuals do appear to vary in areas of misconception, extent of misconception, and the degree to which misconceptions are tested and modified based upon new experience. This conclusion can be applied to problems in living.

PROBLEMS IN LIVING AND FAULTY CONCEPTUALIZATION

A common referral for therapy is an individual, usually a woman, sometimes described as a "doormat personality" because she lets others walk over her. Her encapsulated history may begin with rearing at the hands of an abusive father. From socialization and, perhaps, from her father's statements, she has some understanding that "fathers are good." Besides, how can she feel good about herself if she sees her father as bad? Having little ability to take care of herself independently of family, she is, of necessity, inclined to see him as at least minimally caring, to avoid the greater anxiety associated with the alternative. Having limited verbal fluency, she possesses only a poorly symbolized impression of the following logical syllogism:

Father is good.

Father beats me.

Therefore, I must be bad and deserve it.

She begins selectively attending to phenomena that confirm this false hypothesis. For example, she interprets father bringing home his paycheck as good. She minimizes his inattention to the needs of the family, and his regular weekend binges. Perhaps, in a burst of desperate creativity, she defines drinking as his chosen method of respite from her badness. She looks for confirmation of her badness in her interactions with others and finds them everywhere: at home she tells herself that she should stop father from abusing mother, at school she interprets the teacher calling upon another classmate as a reflection of her own low worth. She occasionally becomes ill and interprets this as God's punishment for her. Well days, being oversaturated, are ignored. With passing years she becomes increasingly unsure and unassertive. So undeserving does she see herself that she is overly solicitious of others, giving more and more and asking less and less in return. She tells herself, "If I treat them nicely maybe they will overlook my badness and treat me nicely as well."

However, the more she gives without demanding anything in exchange, the less deserving she sees herself and the more contemptuously others behave toward her for being so easily pushed around. As this style solidifies with time and practice, exploitively prone individuals are attracted to her "something for nothing" offer. When they offer little in exchange for what they take, she interprets this as proof of her worthlessness. Therefore, she gives even more the next time. Eventually, she marries an individual much like father. After years of abuse she separates and moves to a women's shelter. Much to the consternation of the shelter staff, she returns to her husband. Her maladaptive model of the world has become self-fulfilling or functionally autonomous.

Many problems in living have their bases in faulty conceptualization that is a predictable outgrowth of the interaction of experience with normal organizational phenomena which begin at sensory and perceptual levels and continue at cortical levels. This interaction contributes to an upward spiral of mastery and productivity or to a downward plunge toward debilitation and despair. Earliest concepts are formed in childhood when individuals are least able to evaluate and organize them realistically and are most vulnerable to being overwhelmed by extraordinary experience. As in the example, many go through life believing they do not deserve better.

Many faulty self-concepts at the conceptual level appear to be achieved in a manner similar to the highly serviceable processing strategies at the sensory, perceptual, and interactional levels. The processes of selective attention, deletion, overgeneralization, distortion, and saturation may contribute to a frequent faulty conclusion that "if some is good, then more must be better." For example, with the abused wife, while some humility is self-enhancing, more becomes self-effacing. It may be better to give than to receive, but when she continues to give without getting a fair exchange she teaches herself to see herself as valueless and teaches others the same lesson.

Another example is that of the "overachiever" whose continual striving for improvement or accomplishment overtakes his resources with the result that the individual is debilitated, overstressed, and exhausted. In still another, a degree of helpful planning is overshadowed by such overrehearsal that the individual is seldom spontaneous. Another example of the same form is that of the individual who is empathetic to the extent that he becomes immobilized for fear of the effects of his actions upon others. Other examples will be met within this book and the interested reader may wish to consult Watzlawick (1978) for further discussion of similar phenomena.

ALLEVIATING SYMPTOMS THROUGH CONCEPTUAL CHANGE

Changing one's conceptual model of the world in order to alleviate symptoms appears to be a highly regarded and frequently used step in successful psychotherapies. Prochaska (1979; Prochaska & DiClimente, 1982) studied 18 different "leading" psychotherapies for processes of change. He identified five processes of change common to all therapies, although the approaches varied on emphasis given to a particular process. The psychotherapies also differed on whether the processes were applied experientially or environmentally. Environmental application corresponds closely to what has been described earlier as indirect sources of experience. Related to consciousness-raising, interventions that are environmental include verbal instructions and bibliotherapy, among others.

Consciousness-raising proved to be the most frequently applied change process in 16 of the 18 psychotherapies. Other change processes Prochaska identified were catharsis, choosing, conditional stimulation, and contingency control. Consciousness-raising increases the information available to individuals in order to allow better discrimination. Experiential consciousness-raising is described by Prochaska as "feedback" and environmental consciousness-raising is labeled "education." An important source of feedback across therapies using consciousness-raising has been information regarding "cognitive blinders" that inhibit effective change. These cognitive blinders identified by Prochaska can be understood as conceptual blocks that impede reorganization at the conceptual level and change at the behavioral level.

Whether reorganizing one's interpretation of experiences or providing information (adding new information to one's interpretations of experience), each mode of consciousness-raising of course seeks to modify faulty conceptualizations toward more realistic ones. Frequently the client's reconceptualization of experience takes the form of the particular therapeutic conceptual model to which the client has been exposed in order to reinterpret symptom causation, maintenance, and alleviation. For example, a psychodynamic therapist would be more inclined to help a client reinterpret experience in terms of inner forces that motivate behavior. A Rational-Emotive therapist, on the other hand, would be more likely to interpret self-defeating behavior as responses to irrational ideas, and to apply modifying formulas to eradicate irrational thinking. Regardless of the way the client's consciousness is raised, it is assumed that the client's original understanding of symptoms is not productive because the symptoms are distressing and yet continue to occur.

Consider the example of a young woman who complains of rejection by others and of not being taken seriously. Feedback from her peer group to "be yourself" has not proved useful. The therapist may notice a rather flippant style of relating that invites others to see her as unreachable, uninvolved, and unaffecting. The client may not recognize her flippant style as a problem and may even regard it as a protective reaction to rejection rather than a precursor which is predictive of rejection and minimization by others. Her therapist may notice that the more offended she feels, the more she goes in for superficial banter. The more she behaves in this manner, the more offensive she is to others and the more put off they become. An insight-oriented therapist may attempt to help her break this vicious cycle by helping her to see the pattern as it is replicated in their relationship. Then she is helped to generalize from this relationship to others outside of therapy. A more educational approach may focus on teaching interpersonal skills and self-affirming statements. Each works in different ways to help her achieve more satisfying outcomes. For either to be successful, the young lady must come to see what she originally regarded as self-protective ("If they would accept me I wouldn't act so flip") to be self-defeating ("If I didn't act so flip I would more likely be accepted") before she will decide to implement new untested behavior instead of her tried-but-untrue compromise solution.

If reconceptualization of one's experience is frequently a necessary first step to significant and lasting change, regardless of the therapist's psychotherapeutic orientation, then what are obstacles to reconceptualization? What are intervention strategies independent of a particular professional persuasion that promote reconceptualization and decrease resistance? The remaining chapters of this book will be devoted to these issues. At this point, why faulty conceptualizations are not self-correcting even in the face of disconfirming evidence will be examined.

WHY FAULTY SOLUTIONS ARE PERPETUATED

While organizing processes predispose individuals to occasional misconceptions, most have enough corrective experiences through socialization and individual pursuits to resolve major incongruities between the evidence of their senses and their models of the world. However, some of the corrective experiences themselves can be faulty.

Many of the inaccurate corrective experiences go by the name of "common sense." Hayakawa (1972) reminds us that common sense is "that which tells us the world is flat" (p. 27). Common sense is the reservoir of currently accepted conventions that are accepted as universally true. Because many common sense statements are quite true, and most have great practical utility, it is little wonder that individuals tend to generalize accuracy to all common-sensical statements. It is easy to forget that they are products of only a particular slice in time and are only representative pieces of information that may not apply to all contexts. For example, during the seventeenth century it was thought that the brain operated like a pump. During the industrial revolution, the model was updated to that of a machine. With the advent of mass communication, the model of the brain became analogous to a switchboard. Now the brain is thought to act like a computer. What next?

Like the macrocosmic cultural conventions to which they are related, individual models of the world can contain a great deal of common sense that may have outlived its usefulness. Similarly, conventions offered by parents and other authorities can be mistaken or become outdated. Furthermore, the influence of others can be exploitive even when offered as helpful. Nonetheless, these concepts help inform a person of possibilities and impossibilities, relevancies and irrelevancies, rights and wrongs.

Initial attempts at problem solving are almost always within the boundaries of one's established model of the world. If the attempted solution works, the common sense has practical utility. If it does not relieve the discomfort or solve the problem, the individual is likely to visit with other purveyors of common sense (family, friends, preachers, self-help books) to see if he has overlooked something.

Watzlawick, Weakland, and Fisch (1974, ch. 1) have referred to attempts to change within one's current system which itself remains unchanged as first-order change. When these attempts fail, one has the familiar "beating my head against a brick wall" sensation. Second-order change, on the other hand, changes the system (model of the world) itself so that, if successful, it removes the brick wall altogether. For example, a young man is desirous of making friends. Well-wishers convey sensibly enough that if he is "nice" to others, they will become friends with him. Therefore, he engages in all manner of ingratiating maneuvers. When the initial efforts fail, he simply redoubles his efforts by constantly agreeing with others, performing unsolicited services, presenting gifts, and refusing reciprocation (even expressions of gratitude), and generally being "on call" for others. Watzlawick and his colleagues would refer to this approach as "more of the same" error, because the young man is trying only many forms of ingratiating behavior instead of changing the ingratiating approach itself. In this case the solution becomes the problem because the ingratiating maneuvers tend to alienate others. Only by treating himself more respectfully will he gain more respectful treatment. By giving others a chance to give as well as to receive, the mutuality necessary for friendship will be achieved. By honesty, rather than flattery, he can hope to establish a foundation for intimacy. By allowing others the opportunity to care for themselves, the basis for equality and privacy will become established. These reconceptualizations of friendship and kindness are second-order changes as the concepts themselves are redefined.

Increasingly, psychotherapies are gearing to encourage second-order changes in faulty client conceptualizations. Perls (1969, pp. 27-43) anticipated the perpetuation of client difficulties through first-order change attempts and problem resolution through second-order change to the extent that he named his therapy Gestalt (pattern) therapy. He believed dysfunctional behavior is maintained by attempts on the part of clients to solicit support from others rather than to learn to become more self-supporting. The central axis of his strategy was to enable clients to shift from engaging in more varied attempts to compel others to care for the client (first-order change) to helping the client learn to become more self-supporting (second-order change). The family "system" therapy movement (e.g., Haley, 1976) conceptualizes individual problems as symptomatic of inappropriately functioning family organization that, once modified, obviates the problem behavior. For Perls, Haley, and many other innovative therapists as well, the focus of therapy has been to undermine faulty premises so that more realistic concepts may form, thus allowing more flexible problem resolution.

What appears to separate the problematic from the non-problematic individual and the successful from the unsuccessful therapist is having enough flexibility in world and therapy models, respectively, to reconceptualize when first-order change attempts are not successful. This quality, of course, is what separated Einstein, Galileo, and other bearers of scientific breakthroughs from their contemporaries. None felt bound by the conventions of their scientific societies and, by stepping outside of convention, were able to establish radically new conventions.

INFORMATION-PROCESSING STRATEGIES AND "BREAKTHROUGHS"

If one's model of the world is permeable enough to admit new input, then the same phenomena that result in self-perpetuation of faulty solutions in other more rigid models can result in self-correction and appropriate modification of one's own model. It may well be that flexibility and self-correction provide a fertile ground for unique combinations of material, the synthesis of which we label "breakthroughs."

Left and Right Hemisphere Processing

This new pattern-making ability is thought to be related to emphasis given by the right hemisphere to interpreting data (e.g., Deikman, 1971; Nebes, 1978; Bertelson, 1981; Bruner,

1962; Buzan, 1976; Wyke, 1981). Each hemisphere appears to be primarily responsible for providing one of two major ways of manipulating sensory, perceptual, and conceptual data. (While evidence for this relative bifurcation is mounting, the two hemispheres work in unison. Even if the dichotomy of function does not prove to be sustained at the neurological level, the hemispherical dichotomy remains a useful analog for explaining two ways of handling experience.) The left hemisphere appears to be particularly adept at analyzing data into smaller and smaller parts, whereas the right hemisphere emphasizes synthesis of discrete parts into unified wholes. The left hemisphere is more informational and verbal; the right hemisphere is more imaginative and rhythmic. The left hemisphere specializes in step-by-step processing, as in following a recipe; the right hemisphere specializes in simultaneous processing of several elements at one time, as in orchestrating. The left hemisphere finds differences in similarities; the right hemisphere finds similarities in differences. The strengths of one hemisphere appear to be the weakness of the other. The logical left hemisphere sacrifices the larger picture in favor of detail. The right hemisphere, on the other hand, sees the larger picture well, but may have difficulty distinguishing the real from the imagined.

The left hemisphere appears to be most relevant for learned laws of cause and effect, rules of logic and mathematics, and accumulated facts. The right hemisphere is more sensitive to impressionistic and intuitive sequences of thought. Each emphasis is valuable; the two in cooperative combination can give an individual a highly polished and adaptive world view.

Consider the following demonstration of right hemisphere and left hemisphere knowing. Pause briefly and write a definition of thinking before reading on. Most individuals discover how difficult it is to express this concept verbally. Knowing without necessarily knowing in words is a right hemisphere ability. An individual has increased flexibility in the use of this knowing if one can also encode it verbally. Many individuals who attempt verbally to encode their understanding of thinking resort to restatement ("thinking is having an idea"). Others solve the problem analogically ("thinking is like using computer software"). The exchange of one symbol for another is mostly left hemisphere processing; finding an analog is mostly right hemisphere processing. Now look at the subject, rather than the structure, of your definition. Did you describe both logical and intuitive forms of thinking in your definition? Many individuals who do not give a redundancy ("To think is to ponder") tend to weight their answers toward left hemisphere functioning ("to reason," "to deliberate") and eschew right hemisphere possibilities ("to imagine," "to envision").

To try another experiment: Most readers will have had formal training in learning theory. List the four major types of learning, beginning with classical conditioning, before reading on. Most individuals list operant conditioning. Many others will add modeling as a third type of learning. Did you include insight learning? Individuals, of course, do learn by contiguity, by rewarded practice, and by imitation. Individuals also discover new relationships by recombining previously arranged ideas in new ways. Yet, this learning strategy is rarely treated in depth by learning theory textbooks. Why?

No doubt several reasons account for this de-emphasis of insight. One possibility to be isolated here is that of cerebral hemisphere bias. Our highly verbal and information-oriented culture (Naisbett [1982, pp. 11-38] even labels current U.S. society as the "informational age") appears to favor left hemisphere processing to the detriment of right hemisphere processing. The trend is not new in western culture. Words borrowed from other languages that denote "right" and "left" have acquired pejorative connotations, often for the most innocent of reasons. For example, "gauche" from the French and "sinister" from Latin both signify "left" whereas "adroit" (French) and "dexterity" (Latin) are derived from words for "right." "Right" conveys correctness, straightness, and truth whereas "left" implies untrustworthiness or negativity as in "left-handed compliment." Most equipment is prepared to accommodate right-handers. This is not a conspiracy against left-handers; there are simply far more right-handers. As many as 90 percent of all individuals are right-handed (left hemisphere dominance) and half of all remaining lefties are also dominant in the left hemisphere.

A price is paid for this bias. Information-processing strategies associated with the left hemisphere are particularly adept at taking care of the day-to-day business of living within one's model of the world, but relatively inflexible in recombining experience in new and different ways. When the volume is turned down on the right hemisphere, experience processed by the left hemisphere appears to be more inclined to confirm one's current model of the world by assimilating new material into it rather than rearranging one's model of the world to accommodate new data or rearrange current data. The price of enhanced stability appears to be inelasticity. (The price of right hemisphere overemphasis would appear to be ambiguity, because of its tendency to shun detail and specifics.) One continues to have flexibility within the system, but the system itself becomes more solidified. When the error is the system itself, the person is likely to become stuck. Stability does not necessarily imply accuracy; one can be precise and be precisely wrong. For either hemisphere and consequent information-processing strategies, more of a good thing does not necessarily make it better.

By way of example, many stutterers attempt to treat their condition by trying harder to talk. Paradoxically, the greater their attempts, the move evident their speech impediment becomes. However, when they switch channels from left to right hemisphere processing by singing, their stuttering vanishes.

Among the obstacles to more creative provlem solving for those with problems in living is one of inflexibility in the conceptualization of issues, and solutions to issues, through overreliance upon information-processing functions associated with the left hemisphere. They are like individuals who "fight fire with fire" on all occasions, while others effectively treat fire by dousing it with water. Highly functioning, creative individuals have been identified as being particularly flexible in conceptualization. It is to these individuals we now turn to identify characteristics associated with them.

CHARACTERISTICS OF CREATIVE AND UNCREATIVE INDIVIDUALS

In his essay, *The Three Domains of Creativity*, Arthur Koestler (cited in Adams, 1974, p. 35) describes creative acts as "the combination of previously unrelated structures in such a way that you get more out of the emergent whole than you put in." Whether the creative act is a new invention, discovery of a new principle, an artistic creation, or attainment of a new level of awareness by a psychotherapy client, the act itself is an epiphenomenon of the creator's way of being in the world. For a description of these characteristics of individuals that facilitate creation, Maslow (1968, pp. 135-145) will be consulted. He describes creative acts as a by-product of states of mind that are relatively free from stereotyping. Creatively prone individuals are relatively free of a priori expectations and tend to form opinions sparingly. They have little fear of ridicule, thus can afford to be open to new experience without censorship. Their characteristically high levels of self-acceptance and independence from the valuations of society promote a tendency to continually explore the world of new ideas. Creative persons are apt to be intrigued by the unknown or mysterious rather than repulsed by it. At the same time, creative individuals tend to question the status quo of accepted beliefs. Furthermore, creative individuals have been identified as spontaneous and expressive to a greater degree than the average person. Finally, highly functioning, creative individuals put their conceptualizations to the test by publicly reporting their ideas.

Highly functioning, creative people appear able to live within their society while also being independent from it. That is, they are able to deal with conventional values and beliefs while also modifying and recombining them. Low functioning, creative people, it should be noted, appear to have fluid models of the world; but they tend toward disorganization rather than true flexibility.

Several exceptional psychotherapists known for their ability to enable clients to change themselves have the ability to help clients reconceptualize difficulties in a manner which is satisfying to the client, yet undermines the current unsatisfactory conceptualization. Each may offer compelling, albeit unusual, behavioral assignments within or outside of therapy to set up new sensory, perceptual, conceptual, and/or behavioral contexts. In doing so, the integrated client emerges from therapy far more than the sum of the aggregate parts of the fragmented self that began therapy.

At the other extreme of the flexibility of conceptualization continuum are individuals who have been described as "mechanical thinkers" (Albrecht, 1980, pp. 38-44). These individuals are described as highly opinionated and with little curiosity to seek new information that challenges their habitual view, a view raised to the level of the "right" one. Others may describe these individuals as ethnocentric, dogmatic, and highly traditional. These are individuals who like slogans to guide their actions. Stock phrases, pat answers, and categorical statements further signify their crystallized and unimaginative conception of the world. They prefer simple distinctions like right and wrong, good and bad, black and white. Their rigid conceptualization limits their ability to give and receive humor. Subtleties of intention and understanding are passed over in favor of snap judgments. Mechanical thinkers are not difficult to recognize because their language reflects their avoidance of degrees of difference, nuance, and shades of gray, in favor of "allness" words: "always," "never," "every," and "none." The descriptions of highly functioning, creative individuals suggest openness to the information-processing strategies associated with the right hemisphere. Hyperconventional mechanical thinkers, on the other hand, eschew reconceptualization and appear to resist challenges to already crystallized models of the world.

Most individuals fall somewhere in between the extremes of creative and mechanical thinking. However, greater flexibility in conceptualization that distinguishes creative thinkers from their less creative counterparts can be learned!

SUMMARY

Individuals have an inborn tendency to organize experience. This organizing tendency operates at sensory, perceptual, conceptual, and interactional/behavioral levels. A component of this organizing tendency sorts, modifies, and filters experience at all levels in order to use optimally one's resources for meaningful organization.

A conceptual model of the world from which strategies are derived to solve problems evolves from this organizing tendency. Flexibility in models of the world is necessary not only to accommodate new experiences, but also to correct the inevitable erroneous conclusions (conceptual errors) that are a by-product of the various forms of selective registration and codification of experience associated with development. These conceptual errors, although a predictable outcome of innate organizing processes and enculturation, frequently interfere with successful problem resolution. An important source of inflexibility in problem-solving strategies is overreliance on the styles of processing associated with the left hemisphere. Highly functioning, creative individuals, on the other hand, have personality characteristics that facilitate access to problem-solving strategies associated with optimal input from both hemispheres. As a result, these individuals derive original conceptualizations that result in ingenious applications to practical problem solving.

Many individuals suffering from problems in living resemble conceptually stultified individuals whose revolving-door strategies to resolve reality issues actually inhibit meaningful change. Many particularly effective therapists resemble highly functioning, creative individuals in their great flexibility of approach with clients which leads to positive behavioral changes.

CHAPTER 2

THE STRATEGIC USE OF SOCIAL INFLUENCE IN PSYCHOTHERAPY

Who overcomes by force hath overcome but half his foe.
—John Milton

SUSCEPTIBILITY TO INFLUENCE

Psychological economies are thought to differ in receptivity to anomaly in that less flexible ones are more prone to assume a relationship between new input and current expectations where none actually exists. Providing the novel input is not deleted entirely, it may be made to fit within the existing model rather than the model be modified appropriately to account for the new input. The result can be gaps in the model that are sources of conceptual errors. There is a side to this coin that is an additional source of misconception: a relationship between two phenomena can recur so regularly that the relationship can be assumed to exist on occasions when it does not. If other relevant factors are not also taken into account, the sign can be substituted for the substance. For example, a better quality item is usually more expensive than one of lesser quality although each is used for the same function. Because the relationship between quality and price is usually true, individuals have a tendency to accept the obverse as also being true: a higher-priced item is of better quality than a lower-priced counterpart. Even though better quality of material or workmanship frequently does require a higher price to be charged, simply charging a higher price does not cause a particular item to have improved quality. However, the presence of the implied relationship between price and quality can be highly influential to the shopper who may universally equate higher price with superior quality.

The inferences drawn from a phenomenon and the implication of one phenomenon for another are at the heart of susceptibility to influence. Much of the "magic" of a professional illusionist is accomplished by a related method. The attention of an audience is diverted to one hand or object which is identified as the relevant aspect of the performance while the other hand or another object accomplishes the necessary manipulations to create the effect. The audience cannot discover, much less interfere with, the outcome of the trick, because their attention is focused in the wrong place. In like manner, influence strategies use the natural proclivities of an individual to assume associations that do not necessarily exist in order to steer the person in desired directions, often in a manner that is outside the awareness of the one being influenced. In the hands of an unscrupulous manufacturer, this tendency can be used to increase profit margins by exploitation of the consumer. In the hands of a psychotherapist whose interest is in helping a client achieve agreed-upon goals, the tendency can be used to supplement interventions that, like an alloy, become stronger for the combination of the intrinsic worth of the intervention and the individual's susceptibility to influence.

PRINCIPLES OF INFLUENCE IN CONSTRUCTING INTERVENTIONS

In his important book about compliance to forms of influence, the social psychologist Robert Cialdini (1984) identified six of these nonspecific factors that can be manipulated in a variety of situations to influence an outcome. To these factors he has given the labels reciprocation, commitment and consistency, social proof, liking, authority, and scarcity. As these are the very principles relied upon by professional compliance practitioners in our culture, it is no surprise that Cialdini studied salespersons, professional fund-raisers, advertisers, and even con artists, among others, to isolate these factors of influence. These factors, summarized below from his book, will be seen to be particularly pertinent to innovative ways of dealing with resistance (see Chapter 6). Much can be accomplished, not by attempting to overwhelm the misgivings and misconceptions of others, but by redirecting or misdirecting their force toward more positive ends.

Reciprocal Engagement

Individuals are prone to repay what another has provided them. So motivating is the feeling of indebtedness that "much obliged" is synonymous with "thank you" in our culture. The urge to reciprocate gifts, favors, invitations, and the like can be strong even if the original gift is unasked for or even unwanted. For example, would you seek out one of the apparently homeless "street people" who haunt the inner cities in order to give one of them your change? Even if one asked you for your spare change would you be inclined to give it to him simply because you were asked? But, suppose you were stopped at an intersection and, while awaiting for the light to change, a street person washed your windshield and then extended a hand for change. Would you be more inclined to give something? The pull to reciprocate monetarily is sufficiently strong in many of these instances that unsolicited windshield wiping (even when it is clean) is a spreading practice among these individuals. The benefactor-before-beggar tactic is used extensively because it is so effective. It is an integral part of the "free sample" approach of advertisers and the business lunch of professional lobbyists.

Cialdini has identified an important aspect of the reciprocation strategy that gives the initiator extensive influence over the actions of the one to whom it is applied. Since the initiator chooses the indebting first favor and the nature of the debt-cancelling return favor, he is in a position to request a payoff that differs in type and degree. Consider the study of Regan (1971) used by Cialdini to illustrate. Subjects were divided into pairs and asked to rate the quality of some paintings as part of a study of "art appreciation." However, the other member of each dyad was an assistant of the experimenter and the true interest of the study was the effect of performing a favor upon future compliance. At a particular point during the ratings, the assistant would ask the subject if the individual would do him a favor by buying some raffle tickets, the more the better. Regan discovered that the assistant was able to sell twice as many tickets if the request was preceded by a seemingly innocuous act on the part of the assistant that was unrelated to the raffle tickets. The act consisted of leaving the room during a break and returning with two Cokes, one for the assistant and one for the subject. (For a control group, the assistant would simply leave the room for a few minutes and return.) By performing a small, unsolicited favor the assistant realized a return on investment that was 500 percent greater than that accomplished simply by asking for a purchase of tickets. Could unexpected and unsolicited acts of caring on the part of a therapist create a context whereby the client feels obliged to return the favor through improved functioning? Considerable anecdotal data suggest that this is exactly the case.

Taking Clients from Small Commitments to Great Changes

Once individuals make a choice or take a stand, they frequently encounter interpersonal and intrapersonal pressure to behave consistently with the commitment. This tactic is frequently observed in the foot-in-the-door approach to selling. Small commitments build one upon the other until the weight of commitment changes the conception of the self. Therapists, of course, frequently request small changes on the part of the client that the client is willing to perform in the hope that these foreshadow greater changes and increased commitment to goal obtainment. With each change the client is thought to define himself as a person who can make progress towards becoming his potential self.

The power of a small initial commitment to later compliance is attested to in an experiment by Freedman and Fraser (1966). A researcher who posed as a volunteer worker requested homeowners to allow a large public service billboard reading "Drive Carefully" to be placed in their front lawn. Not surprisingly, 83 percent of the residents canvassed refused. However, a 76 percent compliance rate was achieved with other residents in the area if the major request was preceded by a small one just 2 weeks before. At that time, residents were asked to display a three-inch-square sign reading "Be a Safe Driver." What accounted for this difference between groups when asked for a larger expression of citizenship? Apparently, the small commitment to driver safety changed the view these individuals had of themselves. After agreeing to the unobtrusive request, they saw themselves as civic-minded individuals who valued public safety. Later, they were more inclined than their neighbors to comply with a request that was consistent with their modified self-images.

Cialdini (1984, pp. 83-106) has identified four variables that give the commitment factor its powerful impact upon one's view of self. The first is activity. A person's behavior is a source of information for the individual about himself. Views of oneself can change to coincide with one's activity. Therefore, active commitments are more influential than passive ones. Second, public declarations tend to evolve into more lasting commitments than those made privately. The third is effort. The more energy that goes into a commitment, the greater its influence upon one's conceptualization of self. Initiation ceremonies of all sorts appear to appeal to these principles to bond an initiate, as well as the final one of inner choice that is thought to be the most powerful of the four. Successful salespersons know that the best way to make a sale is to arrange for the customer to sell himself. Individuals who take responsibility for the commitments they make are far more likely to bring their behavior into conformity with them.

The value of inner choice in treatment can be seen in the operation of an inpatient program for substance-dependent young adults directed by William Griffith (personal communication, 1985). Many new residents enter under duress and with a "me versus you" attitude that dares the staff to make the resident cooperate with the program, much less refrain from further drug use. The problem is perplexing to staff who do not want to expel the resident from the program because a return to drug use is highly likely for those who do not complete the program. Yet, to tolerate continual flouting of reasonable rules is an enabling response that replicates the actions of parents who have allowed the dependency to progress. Griffith meets privately with these individuals for a few minutes. Afterward, very few leave the program and most oppositional behavior ceases. What are the points he stresses in this meeting? They are but three in number:

1.   Your behavior tells me you don't want to be here.
2.   Tell me this is so and we'll take you home.
3.   There will be no hard feelings.

A conceptual shift is evoked in the resident from drug habilitation forced from the outside to an internal decision to stay in treatment.

It is thought that lasting changes in the worldview of any psychotherapy client are likely to be accomplished in a psychotherapy structured to provide active participation in a treatment plan that requires that nominal or innocuous changes be followed by changes requiring greater effort toward goals to which the client agrees.

Applying Social Proof to Foil Uncertainty

Individuals are apt to view a behavior as more correct or permissible to the degree that others are seen performing it. Television laugh tracks take advantage of this tendency to increase viewer appreciation of situation comedies. A marginal joke appears funnier if others are heard laughing. It is as though viewers are offered reassurance that they are correctly interpreting lines and actions as humorous. Generally, the more ambiguous the situation or uncertain the individual, the more likely the actions of others are to be accepted as correct, especially if the other people are perceived as similar to themselves.

The desensitizing influence of watching others perform a desirable, albeit anxiety-engendering, activity that is to be imitated is a time-honored element in behavior change attempts (Bandura, 1966). The principle of social proof and modeling can also be applied directly to the relationship between therapist and client. An apparent paradox must be hurdled for the tactic to be most successful. How can a therapist be similar to an uncertain client in order to optimize conditions necessary to evoke the influence of social proof while also modeling different behavior for the client to imitate? One possibility is for the therapist to express empathy and to emulate the client's posture and expressive style before leading the client into more effective behavior. This possibility of pacing, then leading an individual will be explored in more detail in a later chapter.

Therapeutic Uses of Liking

Individuals are more likely to comply with the requests of someone who is both known and liked. Because trust is positively correlated with familiarity and friendship, it is not unlikely for individuals subliminally to suggest to themselves that the presence of one implies the others. People are more likely to go along with the requests of those who are trusted because they do not anticipate exploitation. It would not be a quantum leap on the part of individuals to equate characteristics related to liking with trust itself. Apparently, a second-order inference like this frequently occurs because factors associated with liking have also been found to be associated with compliance (Cialdini, 1984, pp. 167-199). These include physical attractiveness; similarity in personality, background, or life-style; praise, especially if preceded by mild criticism; cooperative contact; and associations with things highly valued (for instance, Chevrolet associates its product with mom and apple pie to promote sales).

As trust is usually a crucial, if not recurring, issue in psychotherapy, systematic application by therapists of characteristics directly or vicariously associated with trust may prove to be highly influential for some clients.

Authority Issues

Stanley Milgram's (1963; 1974) famous (if not infamous) series of experiments demonstrated how powerful an effect obedience to authority can be—to the extent that subjects inflicted what they thought to be excruciating pain upon another just because the experimenter said to do so. Yet, psychotherapy practitioners know the relationship of obedience to authority is not a simple one. Ostensibly, a client comes to a therapist because he is authoritative in the field of behavior change, but may resist or even sabotage the suggested means of goal obtainment. (This topic will be developed in Chapter 6). Generally, both therapist and client alike would prefer for the individual to be neither obedient nor reactive to authority in favor of self-regulation. Therapists who present themselves as possessing such transcendent knowledge that the client need only follow an unexplained directive may solve an isolated problem while unintentionally undermining client self-reflection and self-direction (see Wright, 1985, for further discussion). Alternatively, therapist authority may be used to facilitate the client's creation of a more flexible model of the world of which the process of creative problem solving is a part. One possibility is to use therapist authority to instill confidence that therapy is a means of safely discovering one's resources. To achieve this objective, a therapist frequently desires to directly de-emphasize the authority role while simultaneously arranging the environment in a manner from which the client can infer the therapist's expertise. Through judicious display of the trappings of authority the therapist can appeal both to the client's tendency to be influenced by an authority and the inclination to be self-directing or at least self-concluding.

For example, the usual wall of titles and degrees may be eschewed in favor of one or two summational certificates, ones from which the others are implied (e.g., one cannot earn a Ph.D. without having obtained a master's degree and a baccalaureate so the display of the one allows the client the opportunity to infer the others). Perhaps a postcard requesting a copy of a paper which the therapist has published can be positioned on a nearby desk. A moderately-sized bookshelf can rest atop a credenza. At an opportune moment during a session, the therapist can offer a handout to the client to read and consider. As the therapist reaches into the credenza to get the handout, the client can notice the additional layers of professional books which are hidden within. Afterward, the client schedules the next session with an appointment secretary who offhandedly remarks as much to herself as to the client at the difficulty of finding an opening because so many people consult the therapist. Of course, an opening is found. The authority of the therapist is not forced upon the client from the outside; rather, the characteristic is deduced internally by the client.

Manipulating Access to the Therapist

In the previous section, the remark of the appointment secretary not only implies the value of the therapist to others as an authority who is much in demand, but also underscores his limited availability. Scarcity tends to increase the immediate value of something or someone. The therapist is apt to be seen as more effective by the client simply because rarity is accurately equated with preciousness on many occasions. In a similar manner, a store that announces a "one-of-a-kind" sale with "only one day left" or the consumer's "last chance" for a particular item is appealing to scarcity of the product and limited duration of its availability in the hope of stimulating purchases.

In behavior, the prohibition of an act frequently increases its perceived value. The appeal of any censored material, whether pornography, marijuana, alcohol, or even verbal obscenities may be in part due to this behavioral counterpart of scarcity. Tell someone a product or behavior is unavailable or prohibited and its appeal intensifies. While the increased desire for a prohibited act is a function of reactance, the individual may account for the heightened desire by assigning positive qualities or greater merit to the act in order to account for or justify the increased desire. Thus, a psychotherapy assignment for which the client is only marginally motivated may become more appealing if the therapist requests a delay in its implementation or even prohibits implementation until the client takes a week or more to reflect upon the desirability of the activity. Similarly, the sanctioning of a self-defeating behavior frequently diminishes its appeal.

Cialdini (1984, p.243) reports a consistent finding in the social psychology literature that banning of information is followed by a greater desire to receive it. Another finding is even more intriguing. Censored information is not just more sought after; it also tends to be believed more than material that is freely accessed. The implications for psychotherapeutic communication are impressive. Material that is traditionally kept from the view of the client can become a therapeutic tool when strategically shared with the client. For example, a client who overhears the dictation of the progress note or reads it in the client record is thought to place greater belief in its contents or conclusions than if the material were simply summarized by the therapist. Similarly, an interpretive session for test results can be constructed in a manner that defines it as one where the client is made privy to information usually not shared.

Under what conditions is the scarcity factor most influential? A consumer preference study by Worchel, Lee, and Adewole (1975) suggests two factors to be relevant. Subjects were asked to rate the taste, quality, and worth of cookies from one of two jars. For half the subjects, the sampling jar contained two cookies; for the other half the jar contained 10 cookies. As expected, the rarer cookies were rated preferentially. In two variations of the design, constancy of scarcity and rivalry for the cookies served as treatment variables. Some subjects were given a jar of two cookies from which they could sample. Other subjects were initially given a jar of 10 cookies that was replaced by a jar of two cookies before any could be sampled. Across all ratings, the change from abundance to scarcity created a more positive reaction among raters than did constant scarcity. Apparently, individuals value what is scarce more than what is in abundance, but value even more something that was once plentiful and now has become scarce.

The implications for psychotherapy are provocative. A client initially given free access to the therapist may value therapy more if later sessions are more difficult to obtain, even contingent upon completion of a task or change in behavior. For example, a client usually seen weekly can be instructed to return contingent upon completion of an assignment. A substance-dependent individual who may have been seen frequently during acute phases of treatment can later be allowed to attend follow-up sessions only if substance free. Access to the therapist under these conditions is treated as a valuable commodity to be given in exchange for something valuable to the client—progress toward goals.

Worchel and his colleagues studied rivalry in relation to scarcity by explaining the change from jars of 10 cookies to one of only two cookies in one of two ways. For one group, the researcher explained that the wrong jar was brought forward by mistake and the correct one was being substituted. To another group, the change was described as justified because demand for the cookies was so great that more needed to be made available for others. Those who believed the cookies became more scarce through the process of social demand rather than by mistake were rated the most desirable of any in the study. Competition with others for a scarce item in demand is, of course, what makes auctions profitable and collectibles valuable. This finding can also be applied to the example of scheduling of psychotherapy clients described earlier. A client who shows irregularly for appointments or cancels at the last moment can be rescheduled, not at client convenience, but at a time or day requiring a degree of exertion or inconvenience above the ordinary. The odd hour or longer interval can be justified in terms of leaving peak times of demand available for those who are more regular.

Aside from the teaching power of the logical consequence, when successful it is accompanied by increased sensitivity on the client's part to the importance of the therapist's time as well and a change in perceived stature of the therapist. When therapy time is treated like a commodity that becomes increasingly contingent upon the client working toward goals because it is in demand by other clients, then the value of the therapy hour is manipulated optimally. Therapist skill is required to insure that access is not so difficult as to be interpreted as unobtainable; rather, when successful, it is viewed as a prize within the client's grasp, but one that requires some reaching. Other expressions of caring and concern are thought to be necessary to avoid the contingency being interpreted as a punishment or rejection. The therapist is rejecting the client's failure to keep an agreed-upon commitment and not the client himself.

HELPING CLIENTS MANAGE UNDESIRABLE SOURCES OF INFLUENCE

The psychotherapist's task is a challenging one. On the one hand, a therapist wants unobtrusively to use a client's susceptibility to influence in order to construct potent interventions. On the other hand, a therapist also wants to help a client become less susceptible to disadvantageous influence. Is not one goal antithetical to the other?

Fortunately, this does not appear to be the case. A client can be sensitized to the intrusiveness of influence in his self-defeating thoughts and actions while these same principles are used effectively elsewhere in the individual's therapy. The crucial factor that allows the therapist this flexibility is the absence of client exploitation in the implementation of influencing factors on the part of the therapist. If used sincerely and with no giveaway smirk of self-satisfaction, expression of triumph in double-binding the client, or pleasure in winning over the client's resistance, the individual is unlikely to feel enfeebled, foolish, tricked, or annoyed. Even if detected, therapist and client can relate the communication to client goals and compliment the client on his awareness. More cautious therapists who are concerned about negative reactions on the part of clients can educate them to the factors of influence. The therapist then can request permission to use the principles occasionally to help the client achieve goals, but without telling the client beforehand. In a controlled study, this "informed deceit" gave valid results without upsetting the subject (King & Confer, 1978).

Apparently, individuals expect a degree of deceptiveness on the part of psychologists. If the client does object, he can be asked the objection to making therapy as influential as possible in the client's best interests. Therapists *are* in the business of influencing clients, but doing so without the self-gain at another's expense that characterizes pathological manipulation. Discussion of ways to minimize manipulations in response to application of these principles follows.

Therapeutic Pause

Much of the power of influence comes from appealing to stereotyped responding on the part of the individual. Thus, an antidote to the automaticity of behavior that renders an individual vulnerable to influence is to pause before responding. Defense attorneys frequently counsel their clients to collect themselves and their thoughts before responding to any query on the part of a prosecutor for similar reasons. To do so minimizes the ability of a skillful prosecutor to "put words in the mouth" of witnesses who feel pressured to respond immediately.

Psychotherapy clients can be taught directly to recognize the tactics of influence and their variations (ingratiation, intimidation, threats). By doing so, the pause can be used to disengage from the persuasive component of a particular communication in order to weigh the merit of a particular issue independently of the influence. Self-directed questions intended to perform this function include the following:

> "Regardless of what another wants for me, what do I want for myself here?"
>
> "If I do this, how will I feel about myself afterwards?"
>
> "Are there sources of tension in me that are signaling caution?"
>
> "Where is the evidence to support the claims offered?"
>
> "What could be motivating another to want me to respond in this way?"

What the pause is to an interaction, puzzlement is to a conceptual model of the world. The worldview becomes less trustworthy, more questionable, faulty. The usual ways of responding become less comfortable, more tentative. The individual will likely become inclined to let the model do less automatic reacting while he does more directed thinking. The model itself becomes a candidate for modification.

Making the Covert Overt

Cialdini (1984, p. 224) emphasizes the importance to an individual of asking now another will benefit from compliance to a request. To do so frequently places the interaction in a more complete context, one that includes both parties. This information can be used advantageously to offset the leverage achieved by the influencer simply by commenting to the influencer on one's reaction to what the other is doing.

Consider the commonplace example of a man who invites a woman out to a dinner and show. Later in the evening he may press her for a romantic involvement she does not want. In response to her limit-setting, he may intimate that because he showed her a good time earlier she is expected to return the favor in a sexual way. An appropriate response could be:

"Apparently, when you asked me out for dinner and a movie you had in mind using that to make me feel like I'm indebted to you sexually. That would only be true if you had told me before I consented to the evening that you wanted sex in exchange for the other things. That way I could use the information to guide my decision making. I assume my pleasant company has been sufficient reciprocation. Your pressuring me to do something I do not want to do and don't owe you only leaves me annoyed. I'd like for you to stop while the evening is still enjoyable."

Because it is not possible to know what another's covert expectations are in advance, nothing is owed beyond what is offered at face value. However, potential unpleasant situations can be avoided at times by anticipating the covert demand when one is suspected. In the current example, the woman would have been prudent to have either asked her date what he expected from her in exchange for the evening or to have told him what he could expect from her before either committed themselves to the date.

A Better Map for the Territory

The factor of influence becomes more prominent in a particular situation to the extent that the individual is stressed or uncertain. Susceptibility to influence is also associated with a tendency to make decisions based upon a sample or representative part of the whole of the data necessary to make a correct decision. In addition, the more prone an individual is to allow another to define a situation or relationship instead of doing so oneself, the more likely the individual is to be accepting of interpretations by others within that context.

The same influences that render individuals amenable to well-structured psychotherapy interventions and the hypnotics of commercial influencers are thought to operate in contexts that shape the problems in living as well. Identification of principles of influence to which the client was responsive in the origins of later difficulty may afford direction to the therapist in the construction of interventions.

The stimulation of conceptual changes indirectly through influence is powerful, but not always compelling. Fortunately, a variety of other approaches are available to help individuals construct better maps of their experience. It is to the subject of dismantling unproductive aspects of world models and replacing them with more effective components that attention is now directed.

CHAPTER 3

OVERCOMING CONCEPTUAL BLOCKS TO PROBLEM SOLVING IN CLIENTS AND THERAPISTS

> They see things as others do, but also as others do not.
> —Frank Barron

The first chapter asserts that individuals have routines in thinking to structure the world, to enable them to respond effectively and without delay, and to delimit impinging stumuli by preselecting relevant from irrelevant ones based upon conclusions from past experience. However, these cognitive expectancies can distort new experience to fit the mold of previously held experience and, by doing so, narrow the range of possible responses. The second chapter explained how some regularly occurring cognitive expectancies or routines can be manipulated to influence those who are susceptible. In either case, behavior can become nearly automatic and stereotypical.

DEALING WITH SELF-LIMITING MENTAL ROUTINES

Albrecht (1980, p. 35) offers a demonstration of the effect of mental routines on problem solving. Before reading further,

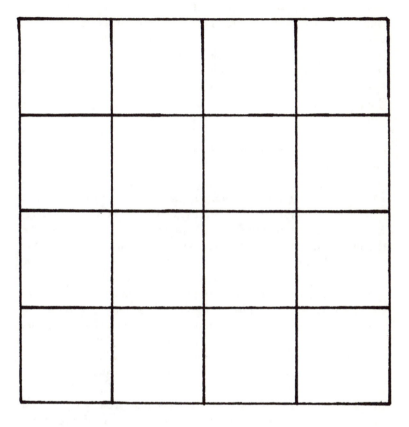

Figure 3.1.   How many squares are there in this figure?

please look at Figure 3.1 and decide how many squares are in the figure.

Most people conclude there are 16 squares in the figure. One's brain tends to quickly organize the information into the obvious pattern of squares. If 2-by-2 squares, 3-by-3 squares, and the large 4-by-4 square are taken into account, a total of 30 squares comprise the diagram. The obvious answer turns out not to be the complete answer.

This tendency to approach a problem based upon a likely pattern evolved from one's organizing tendency does not separate the creative from the uncreative thinkers, clients from non-clients, or successful therapists from unsuccessful ones. All individuals from time to time draw obvious conclusions that are not so obviously wrong and implement problem-solving strategies that are precise, yet precisely inaccurate. What usually separates less creative individuals from their more creative counterparts is the predilection to be locked into these self-limiting mental routines.

Psychotherapy reserves a number of terms and phrases to describe similar uncreative thinking in clients. They may be labeled as being "stuck," "rigid," "constricted," "stereotypical in problem solving," or as engaging in the "more of the same" error. Even the defense mechanisms as postulated by Freud are conceived as maintaining the status quo of the client's psychological economy. These labels reflect the many ways clients deprive themselves of being all that they can be. Therapists, as well, may constrict themselves in their work with clients by applying the same techniques with all clients. To do so may inadvertently require flexibility on the part of the client that taxes his ability. On the other hand, a therapist with greater flexibility can accommodate the client's pathology at first to solidify the relationship before helping the client to make changes.

The purpose of this chapter is to identify limiting mental routines and to encourage readers to develop frames of mind in themselves and their clients that offset them. This is done with the belief that each therapist, regardless of approach, works best by communicating to the client, "If what you are doing is not working well enough, then do something different." And with what do clients respond? Frequently it is with one or more of the following: "It wouldn't be right," "That's not logical," "That's not what my parents taught me," "It's impractical," "It's too uncertain," "I might make a mistake," or "I've never done that before."

These objections are obstacles people place before themselves that prevent them from being more creative in their daily lives. They are of course practiced by clients and therapists alike. In his delightful book, *A Whack on the Side of the Head*, von Oech (1983) refers to these types of conceptual blocks as "mental locks" (see Parnes, 1967, p. 147 for alternative labels).

Einstein once quipped that he began to learn when he forgot everything taught to him in school. He was referring to the tendency of education to teach current convention as if it were the absolute truth rather than the current best guess. In order to be innovative, one questions traditional assumptions. In similar fashion, reconceptualization of problems and solutions to problems begins by challenging the underpinnings upon which current views rest. What may have been true a generation ago can be outdated today. For example, in Freud's Victorian age of formality and overcontrol, a therapy to free impulses "fit." In today's world of greater impulsivity, therapies that emphasize self-regulation and control of one's impulses have come into prominence. What will become relevant in the future will depend upon the cultural context. Having necessary skills to reconceptualize allows one to transcend the context or, more aptly, work within a variety of contexts to solve problems.

The Right Answer Syndrome

Most readers have observed individuals who drink their coffee while driving to work. They are easily recognizable by their juggling antics and occasionally stained clothes. Yet drinking coffee on the way to work is the "right" answer for a number of problems. By driving and drinking coffee simultaneously, one is able to sleep longer, add a warm companion to the routine of the drive, and arrive at work fully alert. While most inveterate coffee-drinking drivers take steps to minimize the negative consequences of their acts of derring-do, others behave as though drinking coffee while driving is the only right answer rather than one of the many right answers.

Beck and his colleagues (Beck et al., 1979; Rush & Giles, 1982) studied the tendency among depression-prone individuals to behave as though alternatives to their particular conceptualization of experiences were either unavailable or nonexistent. They have hypothesized the cognitive underpinnings of depression to be faulty information processing applied to one's concept of self, the world, and the future. Depression-prone individuals tend to interpret themselves, their ongoing experience, and possibilities for the future in highly negative and self-limiting ways.

Because faulty inferences from daily observations are placed within a network of established cognitive patterns for screening and encoding information (schemas), the negative concepts of self, the world, and the future are maintained.

These systemic errors in the thinking of the depressed person that maintain his mistaken belief in the validity of negative concepts (and the exclusion of contradictory evidence) are thought to be widely practiced among clients who enter therapy. Many individuals vary in presenting complaint, but are highly similar in the belief that their particular self-defeating organization of experience is the "only" possible one. Because their accepted conceptualization is ineffective, a sense of despair and helplessness creeps into the client's mental life. The manifestations of demoralization are easily recognizable: personal resources are overlooked, reliance upon others is overrepresented, and effort and participation in therapy is often marginal or ambivalent. At least six related systematic errors in thinking have been identified by Beck's group (Beck et al., 1979, pp. 14-16) as maintaining ill-conceived models of the world. All are reflections of overreliance upon forms of information processing everyone uses daily. A review of these follows.

1. Arbitrary inference refers to a tendency to draw a specific conclusion without sufficient evidence to support the conclusion. For example, a male who is anxious about his sexual performance discovers he is "obsessed" with looking at the crotches of males who pass by him. Despite no history of homosexuality, past heterosexual success, and an active heterosexual fantasy life he misattributes his anxiety in combination with his preoccupation with male crotches to "latent homosexuality," rather than confront the far more likely issue of performance anxiety in his current heterosexual life.

2. Selective abstraction identifies a tendency to focus on a detail independent of its context. Because other mitigating details are omitted, inaccurate conclusions are derived from overrelying upon fragmentary evidence. For example, one woman tells another woman her public-speaking skills are deficient. If, instead of assuming the statement to be true, the recipient were to ask herself what might be motivating the other person to make such a statement, she may discover the intention is to dis-

suade her from competing in order to advance the ambitions of the other person, rather than to render an assessment of the recipient's skill level.

3. Overgeneralizing is similar to selective abstraction. It refers to a tendency to draw a general rule or sweeping conclusion applied to a number of situations on the basis of one or more selected incidents from a single situation. The example of the man who concluded that no woman can be trusted on the basis of his experience with one or a few girlfriends is such a case.

4. Magnification and minimization reflect errors in the evaluation of the significance or magnitude of an event. For example, different individuals may react to the discovery of an affair by their partner catastrophically, as though it were the end of all living, or with such apparent indifference that one wonders whether there were a relationship at all. Each response is thought to reflect a distortion of more moderate interpretations of events.

5. Personalization, like ideas of self-reference, refers to a proclivity to relate external events to oneself without sufficient basis for the connection. Most therapists have worked with insecure individuals who interpret any independent action on the part of their partner as a repudiation of themselves. The result is often a manifestation of the "If you loved me, you wouldn't act that way" syndrome. The implicit demand is one commonly encountered in therapy. Such a client can be interpreted as saying to the partner "my way or no way" since the right/only cure offered for insecurity is to restrict the behavior of the partner.

6. Dichotomous thinking is a tendency to place all experiences into one of two mutually exclusive categories. Such absolute thinking deprives individuals of access to the vast continuum of interpretations between the two extremes. Many clients approach therapy with constrictive models of the world which place experiences into such "either-or" categories. A few examples include "If I'm not in charge, then I'm being dominated"; "If my partner doesn't behave like I want, then he/she doesn't care about me"; "If I'm not abusive, then I'm a wimp"; and "If I'm not a virgin, then I'm a whore."

Watzlawick et al. (1974, pp. 19-20) identify a related fallacy of change: If something is bad, the opposite must of necessity be good. They cite the example of a woman leaving an exploitive husband in order to marry a self-denying one. She becomes deeply disappointed in each marriage, of course, and may believe marital bliss to be elusive, rather than her manner of processing experience eluding.

This common tendency to settle on one possible solution as though it were the one right and only answer is similar to the concept of functional fixedness. Those who are not particularly flexible in conceptualization tend to see things as functioning in one way only and to ignore alternatives. Show a mechanical thinker a handlebar and a bicycle seat and he will show you a handlebar and a bicycle seat. Show the same two parts to Picasso and he will show you the head of a bull with horns (see *Tete de Taureau* by Picasso).

The point is that there are many right answers to almost everything in life. Pause for a few moments before continuing, and think of all the different ways one can avoid spilling coffee while going to work. For most individuals the initial solutions center on manipulating the container for the coffee in order to minimize spillage. For example, one can sip the coffee through a straw, sip it through a broad-bottomed cup, or even fill a cup with a sponge that is then compressed each time coffee is desired. But limiting solutions to manipulating containers for coffee is not in the definition of the problem; it is in the conceptualization of the problem by the solver. One has the options of modifying the stimulant itself (e.g., freeze the coffee into a Popsicle, drink Coke); modifying the form of transportation taken to get to work (e.g., take a bus), or modifying oneself (get up earlier to drink coffee before leaving or be late to work).

Many clients who enter therapy act in problem areas like the traveling coffee drinkers who believe spillage is the price paid to perform alertly. Attempts to solutions are frequently limited to "damage control" rather than to prevention, reconceptualization, or ameliorization. Some may operate at the level of coffee drinkers who develop better containers by finding several different ways to contain distress; but few begin therapy with an understanding of the wide array of solutions and partial solutions before them. So central can become the role of reconceptualization of difficulties and generating alternative problem-solving strategies that Rabkin (1977) has summarized his

Strategic Psychotherapy in two sentences: "Patients attempt to master their problems with a strategy which, because it is unsuccessful, the therapist changes. All the rest is commentary" (p. 5).

Consider the client who solves the problem of making and maintaining friendships by giving a great deal and asking little in return from others. Across a great many relationships he winds up feeling taken advantage of, victimized, and exploited. The client may modify strategies for giving by offering time in one relationship, sex in another, and gifts in yet another. However, until relationships are reconceptualized to include reciprocity, the negative artifacts associated with lopsided relationships are likely to be replicated over and over again.

Almost certainly there is no one cause or no.one solution for any problem in living. Client and therapist alike can look for simple causes and solutions and, by doing so, discover one while overlooking others. Thus, the simplest method of not stopping with the first right answer is to go for the second, or third, or more right answers. If a therapist would but switch from asking questions in the singular ("What does this mean to you?") to the plural ("What are the meanings of this to you?") the client would be sensitized to the omnipresence of multiplicity in etiology and resolution. A client's initial response followed by requests for other possibilities helps the client to create alternatives to his conventional structure for experience.

Think of a client you are working with who suffers from the one right answer syndrome. What can you do about it you have not tried before. What else can you do?

Making Logical Errors

With so much global conflict, some comfort may be derived from knowing that all the civilized world cooperates in the employment of time zones. All agree London is 6 hours ahead of the Eastern Standard Time whether it is morning or night, spring or fall, last year or the next. Such cooperation greatly facilitates international interactions. So reliant are people on the concept of time individually and internationally that it is easy to forget that time is a human creation rather than a discovered attribute of nature. Logic also is not a phenomenon of nature, although logic enjoys wide acceptance and applicability. Logic, like time, is made up by human beings to facilitate operating in the world, rather than something in the world to which everyone must conform.

Hayakawa (1972, p. 200) reminds his students that logic is a set of rules governing consistency in the use of language, not facts about events. Since language is an approximate representation of experience, one can expect difficulty in drawing conclusions from a language about language. In fact, Albrecht (1980, pp. 167-183) has identified 37 possible errors associated with logic. The reader is directed to that source for an exhaustive discussion, since only illustrations of the three major classes from which the 37 possibilities are derived will be summarized here.

The first set of errors relates to arguments, presented as logical, that are not really logical at all. For example, arguments in support of the existence of God may be persuasive and pronounced with great vehemence and carry great allure. Nonetheless, a belief in God ultimately becomes an article of faith and not of logic. The other two major classifications pertain to this kind of error that is actually derived from the system of logic itself.

The first of these sources of logical error has to do with the validity of the premises from which logical conclusions are drawn. That is, logical approaches to any dilemma are only as useful as the assumptions from which logical arguments may proceed. Yet, because life is a process of drawing conclusions from insufficient information, many of the premises of individual models of the world are necessarily built upon articles of faith treated as fact.

For example, most Americans are taught the Judeo-Christian ethic of a just world. We assume the good will be rewarded and the wicked will be punished. This concept of justice is appealingly reasonable: Everyone gets what they deserve. Life experiences that compel an individual to question such fundamental ideals and beliefs about reality are particularly unsettling. Subjection to rape, the contraction of a disabling illness, or even a mugging upsets one's equilibrium and each tragedy requires considerable effort to integrate. Perhaps no life experience is more difficult to come to terms with than the loss of one's young child. Part of grief can be understood as the process of resolving such unwelcome and unreasonable challenges to a personal construction of reality.

Everyone who suffers the loss of a child and comes out on the other side of the struggle is more human and humane. It is akin to the original concept of "soul" as derived by American blacks: to suffer through no fault of one's own and to become more human, rather than vengeful, as a result. Superficial assumptions about the way the world works will no longer suffice. In fact, the word "grief" originates from the Sanskrit "guru" which continues to mean "spiritual guide" even today. All who visit with grief are transformed. One choice is to modify one's model of the world to be more in tune with the evidence of one's experience: Justice is not a "given," but an ideal human beings create, value, and strive to implement. Grief is the risk one takes to live more fully and deeply. The safest life of superficial involvement is also the least satisfying. The child's life can have meaning in the inspiration derived from the loss by those who survive.

Another option is to maintain the faulty worldview of absolute justice and try to fit the experience into it, much like trying to fit a square peg into a round hole. If the grieving parent assumes that "The world is just" is a true premise, then the parent runs the risk of concluding he or she is wicked enough to deserve such dire punishment. Sorrow becomes confounded by self-derogation. Grief can become squandered on bitterness, self-pity, or perpetual mourning. Future experiences can even become distorted to preserve, rather than correct, the faulty premises and conclusions.

The other major class of logical error has to do with the arguments that follow from the premises and preclude the conclusions. Consider an early report that radio waves cause polio. A study found that where radio stations were more prevalent, polio was also more likely to occur. The critical variable that was omitted from the argument, of course, is that of population: Where there are more people there are greater numbers of radio stations and cases of polio. The relationship is one of correlation rather than one of causation.

Some individuals who become clients appear prone to mistake correlation for causation as well. Consider this common example:

> My husband is alcoholic.
> I live with him.
> Therefore, I'm the cause of his alcoholism.

This distressed wife may look for confirmation of her hypothesis and find support nearly everywhere: "Dad was an alcoholic, too. My husband tells me I drive him to drink. I'm not perfect." Well-intentioned friends, even therapists, can join in holding the wife accountable for her husband's drinking. However, symptoms of the spouse of an alcoholic are often best understood as a consequence of living with an alcoholic rather than a precursor that contributed to the partner's alcoholism.

Statistics are an excellent source of distorted conceptualization derived from logical argument. Consider the well-known example cited by Albrecht (1980, p. 180). A pregnant woman went to her physician in a state of extreme anxiety. She had heard that one out of every five children born in the world is Chinese. Since she already had four Caucasion babies, she wanted to know whether the fifth would be an Oriental. An anonymous colleague has identified a widely held expectancy that resembles the statistical concept of regression toward the mean. This individual playfully labeled the phenomenon "pretraumatic stress syndrome" to denote the tendency among many people to believe that, because everything is going so well, disaster must certainly be just around the corner. Because of the logical fallacy, these individuals may feel anxious when stressed, *and* anxious because they are not.

Several therapies address logical fallacies on the part of clients by appealing to reason. The Rational-Emotive Therapy of Ellis (Ellis & Harper, 1975) is a notable and widely practiced method to overcome irrational thinking with near "hyper-logic" and persuasion. Beck's group (Beck et al., 1972, pp. 6-7, 45-61) eschew persuasive techniques in favor of "collaborative empiricism." With this approach, complaints are translated into soluble problems, and dysfunctional concepts are used as hypotheses, the validity of which are tested empirically. The client is allowed to draw his conclusions on the basis of the outcome of these "experiments."

Analogical thinking is a means of making nonlogical connections between things in order to enhance understanding. Take this famous line from a Carl Sandburg poem for an example: "The fog comes on little cat feet." One's left hemisphere knows that fog is not a type of cat; yet, when the line is read, an appreciation of the approach of fog may be more thoroughly obtained. One's right hemisphere finds associations between the two (e.g., quietness, grayness, softness) such that understanding of both cats and fog is richer.

Overreliance upon Rules

Readers may be familiar with the story of the newlyweds who were cooking their first roast. Before putting the beef in the roasting pan, the wife cut off the two ends. Puzzled at her cutting off perfectly good meat, the husband asked his wife why. Without hesitation, she said, "Because my mother always did." When mother was called and asked why, she laughed and said, "I cut off the ends of the roast because my roasting pan was too small!"

Rules *are* helpful in defining ways to operate. They give structure, order, and security. They can reduce anxiety by taking responsibility for decision making out of the hands of whoever is performing the action. They can, on occasion, increase accuracy of prediction and forestall mistakes. Following rules can also place individuals in the position of the newlyweds who thought they were following a rule for cooking roasts. Both helpful and unhelpful rules share in common the ability to inform individuals what can and cannot be exercised—they are sets of options and of limitations. For this reason an important rule is: Rules are made to be broken.

Every family has rules. Not just obvious rules about who does what chores, but also subtle and often unspoken rules that pass along family values, customs, traditions, and rituals. Such rules establish how affection is to be expressed and anger dealt with (see also Satir, 1972, pp. 96-111). Attitudes and ideas about oneself and living are transferred. Some are wonderfully supportive while others are impossible and mutually exclusive. Consider the experience of an otherwise competent woman who suffered panic episodes with great regularity. Her mother had belonged to a particularly self-denying faith and attempted to pass along some of its tenets to her daughter. One idea she passed along was "If you like yourself, you are selfish and egotistical." The more selflessly the client attempted to behave, the more highly (in some ways) she thought of herself because she was living the "right" kind of life. However, this meant she began liking herself, so she could not be selfless without also being selfish. Interestingly, her improvement coincided with coming to see her mother more realistically and not just in challenging the absurdity of her teachings.

Just as almost every major advance in any field occurs when an established tradition is challenged (as in overcoming the "If man were meant to fly he would have wings" mentality), nearly every advance in personal development comes from challenging individual rules and assumptions that are also overly limiting. Consider the successful recovery of a client, Rene, who suffered from multiple personality (Confer & Ables, 1983). She had become the family scapegoat as a child for all the parents' misery. The family had established the rule that all unhappiness in the family was to be attributed to the presence of Rene. This was done in such a way that she was even held accountable for her own conception. The client had spent a lifetime apologizing for herself until she challenged the absurdity of the family rule and came to see her parents and herself in a more realistic light.

Many individuals appear to have a tendency to behave as though rules they have established are inviolate—when nothing could be further from the truth. The nine-dot puzzle (see an adaptation in Figure 3.2) has been used to demonstrate the relationship between cognitive rules and failure to solve problems (Watzlawick et al., 1974, pp. 25-28). The task is to connect all nine circles by using four straight lines without lifting one's pencil from the paper. Before you continue, it is suggested that you attempt the solution. If you are familiar with this solution to the puzzle, try solving it using only three lines.

Were you able to solve it? Most individuals struggle with this puzzle because they attempt to solve it within the field of nine circles rather than extend the lines beyond the perimeter of the nine circles. The rule that the four lines must be within the field of nine circles is in the mind of the problem solver and not in the

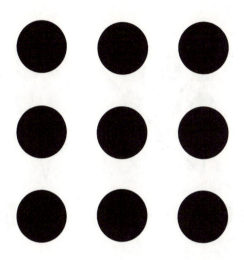

Figure 3.2. The nine-dot puzzle. Without lifting your
pencil from the paper, connect all nine dots
using four straight lines. Then do it using
three straight lines.

definition of the problem. Similarly, the problem can be solved
in three lines if one gives up the rule that the lines must be
through the center of the circles. In fact, one line can be used to
connect all nine circles. Can you see how? All one has to do is
give up the notion that the pattern cannot be cut to form one
row of nine dots (see the solutions in Figure 3.3).

It is possible to make the solution easier to discover by making the problem "harder." That is, if a circle is added on two
ends (see Figure 3.4), the field is broken and, even though there
are more circles to connect with the same number of lines, far
more individuals are able to solve the problem in this form. The
11-dot problem is analogous to many paradoxical interventions
that will be discussed in more detail in Chapter 6. They derive
their power by running counter to expectations that preserve
faulty problem-solving strategies. In doing so, the conceptualizations that maintain the expectations are transformed. A common clinical example is an individual experiencing anxiety at-

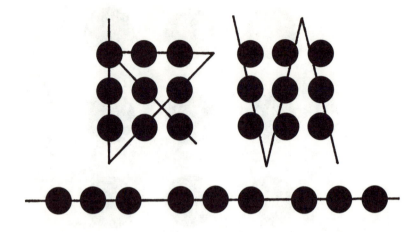

Figure 3.3.   Solutions to the nine-dot puzzle using four, three, and one line(s).

tacks. The client spends much of his energy fighting the attack without success. A therapist may give the apparently paradoxical suggestion to the client to attempt to make the anxiety worse. When the client tries to do so he is surprised to discover that the attack lessens in intensity or disappears altogether. Even though the directive appears to be at odds with the client's desires, it increases congruency by asking the client to accept his anxiety for now and creates an opportunity for the client to take control (through worsening the condition voluntarily) of a state that is experienced as an involuntary condition.

Other examples of severely limiting unchallenged rules include everything from "I don't eat seafood" to "I'm not outgoing." Some may have devastating consequences as in the rule, "If I have a disappointment in my life, I should become suicidally depressed."

Other rules may have been necessary at one time, but have outlived their usefulness. The origin of the standard typewriter keyboard is frequently used as an example of an innovation that has become a hindrance. What possessed the originators of the typewriter to make the top row of letters QWERTYUIOP? The

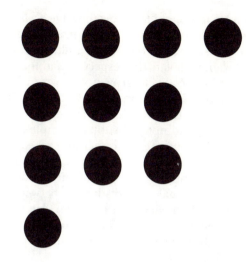

Figure 3.4. The eleven-dot puzzle. Making the puzzle "harder" makes finding the solution easier.

first mechanical typewriters were so slow and clumsy that typists would frequently type faster than the machine could accommodate. The keys would stick and the time taken to free them significantly slowed typists. The solution was to place some of the most frequently used keys in the proximity of the least dexterous fingers. By slowing the typing speed, the process of typing correspondence was actually speeded up. Nowadays, with electric typewriters and electronic word processors, the standard layout retards the pace.

A tendency to live by outdated rules is commonplace among those who become psychotherapy clients. For example, it may have been adaptive for an individual as a child living with abusive parents not to stand up for himself, but the incapacity to do so outside of the home as an adult is severely limiting. A person strictly living by this once functional rule does not give himself a chance to see that the danger is over. Others usually do not assault a person for taking care of himself.

Some out-of-date rules can be maintained for the best of intentions. A client was given some advice about sexual relations from his mother's deathbed when he was eight or so. Problems arose when he attempted to follow the advice when he was in his late teens. The advice, appropriate for a youngster, created a great deal of dismay (not to mention guilt) for this young adult. He did not want to violate the respect he had for his mother, but he also wanted to be able to grow up. He was asked if he would use a road map of Virginia made by George Washington when he was a surveyor to guide him through the state today. He replied that he would not and supplied ample reasons why this procedure would not suffice. His therapist asked if he respected, even revered, the father of our country. He replied that he did. He was able to apply this analogy to the relationship with his mother in order to make the distinction between reverence on the one hand and timeliness on the other. He was even able to believe that, were she on her deathbed today when he was eighteen, she would be unlikely to give the same advice she had when he was a child.

Some rules are helpful to reduce the plethora of options available to individuals; but, too many rules leave persons fixed, rigidly serving the rules rather than using rules to serve individuals. Again, more of a good thing does not make it better. These conceptual conclusions exemplify discouraging and debilitating mottos for living:

"If I ask for something for myself I'm being ungrateful."

"I'm not responsible for the consequences of my actions by virtue of feeling awful about what I've done."

"Showing up for therapy is enough to get me better."

"If I have to ask for something that means they don't want to give it."

"If I can't be happy, I'll make everyone else miserable."

"Someone will take care of me so I don't have to."

By accepting these credos as inviolable, the holder overlooks alternatives to these concepts and many others like them as sources of change. As a result, some may despair at being out of tune with the world while others become increasingly annoyed that the world does not conform to their errant conceptualization.

Another source of limiting rules can be illustrated by adapting a problem posed by Adams (1974, p. 32) in his pleasing book *Conceptual Blockbusting*. A steel pipe, embedded in the concrete floor, protrudes 4 inches. A Ping-Pong ball lies at the bottom of the pipe. The pipe's diameter is only a millimeter wider than the ball so that one cannot use fingers to get underneath the ball. How many ways are there of getting the ball free without damaging the ball, the tube, or the floor and without using any tools other than oneself? Make an exhaustive list before reading further.

No doubt there are many solutions to this problem. A simple solution is to wet one's finger in order to stick it to the ball; then, the ball is easily raised. If given a pitcher of water could you think of another way to retrieve the ball? Most do not even consider spitting or urinating in the pipe to float the ball, but readily apply the same principle when offered a pitcher of water. Cultural taboos are sufficiently strong that these two methods are rarely considered by even the most flexible of thinkers. This experiment replicates the lives of many stuck individuals whose experience has generated models of the world that prohibit from consideration alternatives that would be highly accessible to others who were not exposed to subcultural and family taboos against them. These prohibitions can be as many as there are family eccentricities. A few common examples include the following:

"Nice people don't get angry."

"We don't talk about Mom's alcoholism."

"Let's not discuss that you and I don't like one another."

"Men don't express feelings."

"Women are emotionally weaker than men."

Whether a taboo, or any rule for that matter, is constructive or destructive depends upon the outcome of acting upon it. If the incest taboo were not practiced, youngsters could be readily exploited sexually and mutations from genetic inbreeding would abound. On the other hand, if the taboo against cutting other humans were not overcome, the technique of surgery could not have been developed. Context becomes an important moderating variable in the utility of any taboo.

All people can ask themselves when facing untoward circumstances what outcome they desire. What are some rules that, if followed, would maintain obstacles to the outcome? Are they being followed and, if so, how realistic are they? What rule, if followed, would bring the desired outcome closer? What other rules, no matter how unrealistic, would be helpful in achieving the ends? Can this outrageous rule be used as a stepping stone in some way toward a more realistic approach?

Breaking a rule is a good way to get out of a rut. The author once adhered to a rule that he would complete difficult things first in order to leave the easier things for last. In this way, it was reasoned, the worst would always be behind and better times ahead. By reducing stress in this manner it was hoped to maximize enjoyment. The dishwasher would be loaded from the back forward in order to get the most inaccessible places out of the way first. When a bag of cookies was purchased, the broken ones were eaten first in order to preserve the aesthetically pleasing unbroken cookies to be savored last. Invariably, the dishwasher would be run when it was less than full so the easily reached places remained unused. By the time all the broken cookies had been eaten, the ones that were originally whole had become broken. The rule, subconsciously intended to maximize satisfaction, actually interfered with its obtainment. By breaking the rule (and becoming less obsessive), the author is pleased to report he gets as much accomplished with more enjoyment than before in these areas and many others.

Children, not being well socialized, are not as hindered by self-imposed rules. Unorthodox problem solving becomes part of the child's repertoire. For example, a three-year-old was once confronted with the problem of opening the door to go outside (a feat requiring both hands) while also preserving his slice of bread and peanut butter. Unencumbered by adult norms, he plastered the bread to the wall, used both hands to turn the knob, peeled the bread from the wall, and happily skipped out to play. One way to break from a confining rule, then, is to put oneself in a childlike state in order to free the imagination to solve a problem. To do so removes the complexity of one's thoughts to the extent that an individual may be able to identify a simple yet novel solution.

The following is a problem, derived from the "Kiddie Korner" section of the Sunday comics, to illustrate how some problems are more easily solved by overlooking complexity in favor of a childlike state of mind. Using the following series as a guide, the task is to identify what letter comes next: 1. 0 2. T 3. T 4. F 5. F 6. S 7. S 8. ____.

Adults may find themselves looking for complex alphabetical patterns either in terms of positions in the alphabet or in terms of shapes of the letters to solve the problem. The requested solution is "E." Did you get it? The solution is frequently too simple to be noticed by adults, but is more readily accessible to children. Each letter coincides with the first letter of the corresponding number. "E" begins the spelling of the number "eight."

Because people have to live with the consequences of their actions, breaking rules may be more frequently useful in generating new ideas for reconceptualization than in serving as unmodified plans for action. As an exercise, list the rules practiced in your approach to therapy. What do you think? Are you getting the outcomes you want? Are any of them outdated, taking a longer or more complicated way than necessary, avoiding potential areas of client discovery because you have been taught not to approach those areas?

Practicality Carried to a Fault

Einstein performed what he described as "thought experiments" to help him understand puzzles associated with relativity. For example, he might ask himself what things would be like if he rode in a streetcar going the speed of light. He never intended to actually perform these fantasies. He did not have to. Einstein understood fully that because something is unrealistic that does not mean it is not useful. He used his impractical thoughts as springboards to more practical applications.

Many individuals who become stuck conceptually solving problems in living do so because they do not have a means to suspend their status quo models of the world to explore other options. They behave as though they will be held accountable for whatever they may be thinking so they deviate as little as possible from the acceptable. However, "what if" questions provide a means to suspend rules without experiencing potentially deleterious outcomes. In actuality, individuals are held accountable for actions and not for their thoughts. What follows is a small sampling of possible "what if" questions a therapist may pose to a client:

> "What if you became embarrassed in this situation? What would be so bad about that?"
>
> "If no harm would come to you, what would you like to say to him that you didn't say?"
>
> "What if you weren't shy? What would things be like?"
>
> "What if the worst that could happen did happen—what then?"
>
> "What if you became paralyzed and couldn't compulsively wash your hands anymore? Would the urge still be there?"

Now it is your turn. Write three "what if" questions for each of five of your most resistant clients. Afterwards, ask yourself how you can introduce the best of these questions into a therapy session.

The identical "what if" strategy can be applied to therapists to enhance understanding of clients, to generate testable hypotheses, and to overcome impasses. For example, the therapist could ask himself, "What if I behaved toward the client the way the client behaves toward me?" By asking the rhetorical question, the therapist may predict the client will have a similar emotional reaction to that of the therapist when the client behaves that way. That might suggest the possibility of asking the client how it feels inside to have the therapist behave in such a manner. When the client has fully reported the negative reaction, the therapist can consider the therapeutic impact of offering the statement, "Now you know how others feel when you come across that way. Is that something you want to modify?" Here is a potpourri of other rhetorical "what ifs":

"What if I said nothing the whole hour? How would the client react?"

"What if I took the role of mother or father here?"

"What if I asked the client to exchange chairs today?"

"What if I said the opposite of what I'm supposed to say here?"

"What if I perched on my desk like a vulture when the client arrived?"

"What if I cried here?"

Your turn again. Let any five clients come to mind. Think of three "what if" questions for each and let your imagination run free. You are only held accountable for your actions!

Avoidance of Ambiguity

The Chinese character meaning "crisis" is a combination of two other characters, those of "danger" and "opportunity." This is a stunning psycholinguistic realization that conflicts, uncertainties, and paradoxes are opportunities for growth as well as for loss. They are opportunities for growth because they require individuals to think and behave in new ways to solve the dilemma. A prominent physicist epitomized this sentiment by meeting obstacles with "Thank God, I'm stuck. Now I can learn something!" Yet a frequent unrealistic expectation of clients is that a clear, certain (not to mention easy) way exists to put life in safe perspective, ease struggles, and obviate the need for lifelong self-regulation. Toward the other extreme, General Douglas McArthur once observed, "There is no security; there is only opportunity." While perhaps more an expression of his capacity for hyperbole than strictly a statement about uncertainty, the point remains that increased security frequently works against one's ability to take advantage of opportunities.

All therapists have had the experience of working with clients who, rather than risk the unknown, settle for severely compromising, albeit secure, solutions and relationships. These compromises provide unfulfilling, yet predictable, results. Others both want to be more self-supporting while also holding on to support: "How can I get a man who will take care of me, but not dominate me?" or "I want to be mothered, but I don't want anyone to treat me like a kid."

Each example is a living riddle, a portrait of ambiguity in search of certainty. Yet, the creative synthesis offered by therapy is in integrating disparate parts of selves into higher functioning wholes. What is conflictual at one level is potentially resolvable at another if one will but risk it: The taking of reasonable risks is what appears to separate successful from unsuccessful individuals. How do therapists create opportunities for one client to discover she requires neither domination nor protection from others? Or another client to understand he or she can mother herself or himself? Chapter 6 deals with the subject of clients who settle for safe, but unsatisfying, solutions to life challenges. All interventions derived from that discussion share in common the introduction of uncertainty or ambiguity by the therapist within the context of a helping relationship. Consider the simple, but elegant, directive by Milton Erickson for a client to drive 30 miles into the desert because "something will come to you" that will be helpful. Because it is offered within the therapeutic relationship, the implication is that the discovery will be helpful. Because it will require unusual effort, the implication is that the payoff will be significant. Because the therapist is confident something beneficial will occur, the implication is that something will. For the moment, a sampling of other ways to introduce beneficial uncertainty to the client will be identified:

1. Confronting the client with his inconsistencies is perhaps the most conventional way to introduce ambiguity:

Client: I'm satisfied with myself. . . . I feel like a puzzle with pieces missing.

Therapist: You say you are comfortable and you also say important parts of the puzzle are missing. How do you explain this to yourself?

2. Another type of intervention is to provide unusual or unexpected responses:

Client: It's useless!

Therapist: I wish I could get you to believe that, because then you may begin to take things less seriously.

Client: You sure are a quack.
Therapist: To seek help from an ignorant man like myself, this is crazy (Beier, 1966, p. 53).
3. A third possibility is to introduce an apparent paradox:
Client: I'm more depressed.
Therapist: Maybe you're not depressed enough because when you're hurting badly enough you'll become more motivated to do what it takes to end the hurt.

Client: My mother is always getting me to do things I don't want to do.
Therapist: What do you think of the idea of asking your mother to tell you to do things she knows you won't want to do in order to get practice asserting yourself? You could ask her to be sure to be persistent so you can have plenty of practice saying "No." You could add that you'll do your best to not give in so that her efforts will not be wasted.

Therapist: You think you don't know how to help yourself so we won't be using your thinking today.
4. Metaphorical communication is an analogical approach to providing ambiguity:
Client: I really put one over on these guys. They think I'm the greatest.
Therapist: I have this picture in my head of you riding off triumphantly on the Trojan horse. Can you apply this in some way to your situation?
5. Another possibility is to support or even encourage client resistence:
Client: I don't want people around. I just want to be isolated by myself.
Therapist: You can give yourself a sample of that and see. Would you be willing to go to St. Simon's [a resort island, all but deserted in the off-season] for a couple of days by yourself and see how you like it?
Introducing uncertainty facilitates generating another perspective by undermining current ones. Confronting clients with their own ambiguities keeps them at their growing edge. Think

of a client with whom you have reached a plateau. Sessions may be routine, predictable, even boring. What can you do to introduce a measure of ambiguity into the relationship? What are the possible outcomes? Would those outcomes be useful in breaking the impasse?

Confusing Error with "Wrongness"

Just about every reader will have a degree of mastery over some sport or complex skill, whether it be tennis, sewing, woodworking, poetry, ceramics, etc. None developed these skills errorlessly; rather, with each error of performance something was learned that improved future performance.

Those with models of the world that do not appreciate the informational value of mistakes are likely to take few risks. Because reasonable risk-taking leads to innovation, these individuals are likely to come across as rather rigid, stereotypical, and dogmatic. Spontaneity is replaced by ritual or routine. Deviance from dogma is no longer accepted as different; rather, it is seen as wrong. "People who have to be right, frequently feel wronged" (Bandler, 1980). Those who feel wronged view the other person as the offender rather than reevaluate their own premises. The rigidity is perpetuated.

A particularly pernicious mental routine is one that conceptualizes success and failure as opposites instead of viewing each as a necessary part of the process of producing outcomes that lead to mastery. Individuals become more proficient at tennis by playing others who are equally or more skilled rather than those who are easily defeated. Because errorless performance is unrealistic, quitting is probably best understood as the opposite of success in a variety of contexts. Edison knew this well. He performed thousands of experiments to find a workable filament for his light bulb. He tried everything from fishing line to bamboo before settling on carbonized cardboard. All the refinements that have come since may be attributed to not enshrining cardboard as the "only" filament. Edison was a believer in the principles that the products of genius are unrelated to quitting, but strongly related to persistence—and perspiration. No one can take perseverance from an individual; the individual can only give it away by giving up.

What are some of the ways therapists have attempted to help clients reconceptualize "To err is wrong"? Ellis and Harper (1975, chaps. 10-11) typify the cognitive approach. They identify fear of failure as a form of irrational thinking that they directly attempt to help a client modify through logical persuasion. The rational approach seeks to broaden a client's thinking by separating achievement from worth, identifying the overvaluation of rightness with a desire to excel over others, and enjoining their clients to consider other alternatives to living than "success."

One indirect approach makes use of the therapist as a model. Consider the following statements by a therapist to a client struggling with "To err is wrong":

> "May I have your permission to try something different and see what happens?"
>
> "I may be way off base here, but. . . ."
>
> "I guess I was mistaken about that. Let's see what can be salvaged from my error that is useful."

Each has a way of sanctioning error by acknowledgement of one's potential for mistakes without self-condemnation. If the therapist gives himself permission to make mistakes, the client may learn acceptance vicariously.

By instilling a sense of the absurd or playfulness into one's therapy, the therapist communicates "Life is too serious to be taken seriously." For most, the consequence of play is enjoyment. This approach was offered to a particularly overcontrolled young adult. As he was monotonically describing his inadequacies, the therapist suddenly left his chair and strode around the room. The client was asked if he played golf (which he did not). The therapist requested he stand up and take practice at swinging an imaginary golf club. Befuddlement gave way to amusement and by the time the hour was ended, he was animated and laughing, stating he felt better than he had in a long time. With practice, he was eventually able to transfer his animation to outside the therapy relationship. He is now married—a goal he thought to be an impossibility 2 years before.

Therapeutic uses of humor.   Allied with the absurd is a sense of humor. Practically all therapists espouse the utility of humor; Farrelly and Brandsma (1974, p. 95) make it a trademark of their approach to therapy. An effort will be made here to support humor in therapy from the point of view of its facilitating effect upon reconceptualization. Koestler (1964) has identified comic inspiration as one of the three domains of creativity alongside scientific inspiration and artistic originality. All three share a fundamental commonality he labels "bisociation." He defines bisociation as "any mental occurrence simultaneously associated with two habitually incompatible contexts." The joke teller begins a chain of events that make sense within one frame of reference. The punch line, however, abruptly places all that precedes it into another frame of reference that is surprising and humorous. Arieti (1976) offers a similar formulation of the comic twist: "the subject perceives a comical stimulus when he is set to react to A and finds himself reacting to B, because of the confusion between the identity and similarity of A and B" (p. 115).

A brief joke will be used to illustrate. A pretty young woman approaches the old duffer and, while batting her eyes and thrusting her assets forward, asks him if he wants to play around. Without hesitation, the old duffer eagerly responds, "I'd love to, but where are your golf clubs?" The first part of the joke places the content in the context of a sexual advance; the punch line takes the same material and places it in the context of a round of golf. The conceptual shift produces humor. It is difficult for the listener to be offended or discouraged by mistaking the proper context. He automatically assumed the most logical (and intended) context. The joke turns on its ability to evoke a shift in conceptualization. The conceptual shift on a comedic level is structurally similar to conceptual shifts sought in dysfunctional models of the world among psychotherapy clients. Any joke gives active practice at reconceptualization in a highly nonthreatening manner.

Humor is particularly useful for those conceptually inhibited with error-making because it offers the client the experience of having a mistaken conceptualization, the recognition of which is accompanied by laughter rather than ridicule, belittlement, disgrace, or any other responses that teach one to be phobic of errors. The effect is one of unobtrusive desensitization.

Any joke of the same form as a client predicament can take the edge off a serious topic in such an entertaining manner that the impact may stay with the client more than a serious dialog with similar theme. As an example, the reader is invited to consider how one might relate the following humorous story to a client who requests direction from his therapist and then applies it in a self-sabotaging manner:

Have you heard the one about the guy from New York City who went to the physician because he was overweight? The physician said, "You need to exercise and the weight will come right off."

"But I hate to exercise," replied the man.

The physician responded, "Then take up jogging and build slowly each week. Run 1 mile each day for the first week and 2 miles daily for the second. Then run 3 miles a day for the next 2 weeks. Call me afterwards to let me know how you're doing."

A month later the phone rang in the physician's office. The call was from his overweight patient. "Doctor, I need your help. My muscles are sore all over and my feet are swollen from running."

"Well, drive right over and see me."

"I can't. I'm all the way to Poughkeepsie!" (After a joke from "Laughter, the Best Medicine", 1984.)

The client, asked to relate the joke to his predicament, may develop an awareness that entrusting himself to directives from experts does not supplant the necessity of his actively processing the input and then acting upon it in a self-enhancing manner.

In a hilarious psychotherapy chapter, Farrelly and Brandsma (1974, ch. 4) describe the impact of humor in Provocative Therapy. The therapy may parody, lampoon, even mock, the client's "crazy" ideas or behavior. Traditional therapy or the therapist himself is not immune to the barbs, either. The intention is to provoke the client to clarify thoughts or feelings, to deflate self-pity, to increase tolerance for one's fallibility, or to help a client catastrophize less, among others. They believe that "a humorous presentation not only desensitizes a client's shame and anxiety, but also humorous ridicule and sarcasm sensitizes clients to their own deviancy" (p. 114).

Acceptance of mistakes on the part of client and therapist opens each to the possibility of discovering something different or trying something innovative and seeing what can be learned from the outcome.

Status Quo Thinking

A client very much wanted to relate more effectively to men. She was asked if she had ever thought of wearing makeup. "I could never do that." she said earnestly. "That's not the way I am."

The following may appear to be such a truism as to be mundane. However, the frequency with which it is met by clients as a novel idea suggests it is worthy of repeating. "I've always been that way" is irrelevant to becoming another way. To believe otherwise is comparable to an infant saying to himself, "Because I have always crawled, there is no other way to locomote."

This attitude is not limited to clients. Therapists can limit themselves by saying "That's not my area," or "That's not the way I was taught therapy," or "I don't treat that type of client." Some therapists may indeed be sufficiently satisfied with their areas of specialization or options afforded by their approach to therapy that little need for change exists. Clients, on the other hand, most often come to therapy because of dissatisfaction with themselves. Yet they may defend their status quo vigorously with protestations that to behave differently would be just that —different! Insecure individuals as a whole tend to grip tightly what they have as though protecting it from being taken from them, even though its value is disputable. More secure individuals appear to be more receptive to alternative points of view. Festinger (1957) has made this and similar observations synonymous with cognitive dissonance theory.

Exposing oneself to experiences outside of those with which one is familiar may confirm some cherished beliefs and refine others, but is almost always broadening. A great deal can be learned about psychotherapy, for example, not by reading psychotherapy books exclusively; but by reading in philosophy, etymology, evolution, biography, creative thinking—even learning how to draw. By learning etymology, for example, one becomes more sensitive to the connotations of words. An individual acquires some of the characteristics of an etymologist which in turn can be applied to a therapy approach. In a similar vein, a client's protestations that she cannot wear makeup because that would be phony for her would no longer be true the moment she applies it. She may even discover that wearing makeup is more true of her than the person she had been all her life.

The foregoing discussion is not meant to imply that conformity, tradition, and specialization are wrong or unnecessary. Without conventions and cooperation, chaos would certainly reign. Overreliance upon sameness, on the other hand, does stultify. In the words of von Oech (1983), "When everyone thinks alike no one does much thinking" (p. 113). To the extent that the therapist has a broader perspective than the client, he is well positioned to help the client acquire a wider one as well.

The reader interested in profiting most from the strategy to create and apply therapeutic metaphors to be presented in the next chapters can do so by cultivating interests across a wide variety of fields. To do so will give the therapist more points of contact with individual clients and offer a richer array of experiences from which to generate therapeutic metaphors.

TRANSFORMING CONCEPTUAL FLEXIBILITY INTO ACCURATE INTUITION

The breaking of mental routines opens an individual more fully to his intuition. The intuitive process of having immediate certainty or conviction arrive without active manipulation of experience can be powerfully employed in the service of psychotherapy. Aside from increasing immediacy and spontaneity in the relationship with the client, powerful therapeutic interventions can be derived from the raw material of intuitions. These intuitions and their therapeutic by-products are only as useful as they are valid and used confidently by the therapist. Interventions that are derived from this greater receptivity can be trusted to the extent that the therapist wants to be helpful to the client and desires little in return beyond the contracted fee. That is, a therapist probably helps best those clients who are liked the most and needed the least. It is possible to understand a client so that some of his loveableness is revealed. It is certainly possible for a therapist to have most of his personal needs met in a way that does not exploit a client.

Being able to trust oneself and one's intuitions serves as a necessary counterbalance to the client's self-distrust. As a result, the therapist can have greater ability than the client to comment on experience and, by doing so, raise the level of the relationship above that of social convention. Socially, one would rarely say to an aquaintance, "I'm feeling annoyed right now. Did you know you had that affect on people?" or "I'm thinking you might not come back and I don't want that to happen. What can we do about it?" And yet such statements are commonplace in therapy.

Therapist self-trust in intuition yields courage to counter the client's discouragement and flexibility in problem solving to foil the client's rigidity. To the extent that a therapist trusts himself, he will take more risks, break some rules, look for more than one right answer, tolerate uncertainty, look foolish now and then, and go far beyond the status quo of mediocre therapy. To the extent that these attitudes are conveyed to clients, the same can become true of them.

CHAPTER 4

THERAPEUTIC METAPHORS
Making the Unfamiliar Familiar

To go exploring
And at the end of all our exploration
To return to the place we started from
And discover it for the first time.

—T. S. Eliot

USING METAPHOR TO FACILITATE INSIGHT

Susan was a thirty-eight year-old divorced woman referred by her supervisor because of excessive mistakes in her work. Since she was an assistant physical therapist at a hospital, some of her mistakes were potentially life endangering. At first meeting, the client was very tense and anxious. Facial tics, blinking, and crying punctuated her recital. She reported that at work, "Everyone asks me for help and I want to please every one of them, but I've got my own work to do and when I try to do it I make mistakes. Last week my supervisor told me if my work did not improve, I would lose my job."

She summarized her interpersonal relationships, "I always want to do the fair thing, but for some reason I always end up being taken advantage of or being walked over." She had been married for 20 years before getting a divorce 4 years ago. For the last 6 years of their marriage her husband would "verbally cuss me out in front of the children. And I felt like he was having an affair which was going on for about a year, though I didn't have any proof. But I really didn't want to find out any proof, either." The client stated that she had not attempted to establish a relationship with another man since then because she was fearful of getting too close.

The client's dilemma was understood to be one of treating others' comfort and convenience as though it were more important than her own comfort and convenience to the extent that she was doing all of her work and much of that of her coworkers as well. This effort taxed her resources to the point that she developed symptoms and jeopardized her job. This hypothesis was tested by asking her how she would respond to a request of a patient she sees for physical therapy during the day to come to her hospital room after normal working hours. The request included the demand for a rubdown in order to relieve pain. Susan replied that she would probably go up to the room as requested in order to attempt to alleviate the pain of the individual.

Since the hospital employs night personnel to perform all necessary functions, the remainder of the therapy hour was spent attempting to help Susan understand that when she treats someone else's pain as if it is more important than her free time (when other staff are available), she sets herself up to be used by others. Her therapist explained that when she attempts to relieve somebody else's pain at all costs, even at great expense to herself, she is the one who winds up hurting and less able to provide help during the hours she is responsible to do so. He added that it would be helpful for her to distinguish between unreasonable and reasonable requests and that when she treats an unreasonable demand as though it were a reasonable one, it teaches others to take advantage of her. Further, when she treats herself as if her time is not as important as someone else's, she teaches others to take advantage of her. Finally, her therapist pointed out to her that when she gives away everything she has without getting something back she winds up with nothing. Why should others treat her more respectfully when she treats herself so disrespectfully?

How far did logical persuasion get her to redefine her conceptual errors? Not far. The next week she was asked to summarize the previous discussion. She said that what she got from it was for her to be a "mean ole person."

At a future session an exchange quite similar to the following occured:

Therapist: Susan, suppose you were in line at a grocery store and a person came up behind you in line with an equally full cart of groceries and asks if she may go before you in line because she's in a hurry and her time is valuable. Let's assume you're buying your groceries after work and you're tired and eager to get home. How do you react?

Client: Well, for her to ask it must be pretty important and I wouldn't know if it were an emergency or something so I would probably go ahead and let her go first.

Therapist: How do you feel about yourself giving in?

Client: If she were rushing because of an emergency I don't think I'd feel bad about it.

Therapist: Are you aware that you're assuming an emergency on her part, rather than her having told you? (pause) If people have an emergency, do they go shopping?

Client: No. I guess I am assuming a lot.

Therapist: What do you think will happen next time you're in that line and she comes up behind you?

Client: Well, I guess she'll ask me the same thing.

Therapist: That's right, you've taught her that it's okay to request you move over so she can convenience herself. Is that what you intend to teach?

Client: No.

Therapist: What do you think she thinks of you?

Client: I'd like for her to see me as kind of generous, but she likely sees me as kind of a sucker.

Therapist: Is that the way you want to be seen by others, as kind of a sucker?

Client: No.

Therapist: And isn't that what brings you here, this very kind of thing at work and in other situations, feeling more pressured so others can feel more at ease?

Client: Yes, it is. And it really bothers me. But it bothers me not to give what others want, too.

Therapist: Susan, are you responsible for the other person's groceries or is that her responsibility?

Client (after thoughtful pause): That's her responsibility. I hadn't thought about it like that.

Therapist: And if it is her responsibility to take care of her groceries and she's in a hurry, does it make sense to you that she needs to do her grocery shopping at a time when there aren't lines rather than expect you to move over because she's in a hurry?

Client: I hadn't thought about it like that, but I was treating her as though she counts more than me.

Therapist: And how do you suppose you would feel about you when you treat yourself as though you're not very valuable by moving just because someone makes the request?

Client: I guess I do see me as pretty unimportant, but I'm also beginning to see how I do that. Her groceries *are* her problem and not my problem. And if she doesn't want to wait in line to get groceries she needs to come late at night or something.

Therapist: Can you see where else in your life you can see this happening?

Susan was able to associate this issue to her problems at work and in her personal life. The next week she reported being able to deal effectively with the unrealistic demands of a friend to take her shopping. The friend had requested the ride without notice at a time inconvenient to the client. Importantly, Susan was able to say no without feeling like a "mean ole person." This exchange was a beginning for her to be able to treat herself as though she deserves better than she was giving herself before. Soon after, the tics and nervousness vanished. She spontaneously reported that on other occasions of the same form as the story, she would think to herself about the lady in the grocery store and respond in a self-enhancing manner.

Two approaches, highly similar in theme, but strikingly different in structure, were offered to the distraught physical therapist. The initial approach, a highly rational one, appeared on target, but proved to be ineffective. The client heard the message as an exhortation to be cruel to others, an understanding she would be unlikely to implement. How did she derive this meaning from a discussion intended to help her treat herself as respectfully as she treats others? Her understanding of the message is a logical conclusion within her faulty conceptual system which dictates that she is responsible for providing comfort to any and all comers regardless of the toll on herself. The persuasive approach, apparently logical and well formed, had little impact upon her worldview; in fact, the argument was distorted to fit *within* her faulty model of the world.

The second approach, a highly metaphorical one, proved to have far more impact in her case in modifying both her concepts about responsibility and her behavior: a second-order change. How did this happen? The intervention began a step removed from her presenting problem related to her occupation. Talking about a grocery store line, an experience highly accessible to nearly everyone, is far less threatening to her self-concept than discussing her deportment at work. The connection between a grocery store line and her work behavior is an analogical, rather than a directly logical, one. The second approach relies heavily upon the "similarities in differences" ability associated with right hemisphere functioning to penetrate the ingrained worldview and bypasses the logic-seeking left hemisphere tendency. Left hemisphere functioning, as noted earlier, is more prone to modifying new input to conform to current conceptualization rather than modifying current conceptualization to conform to challenging input. Once the analogical connection is made and the initial conceptualization supplanted by a more realistic one, the left hemisphere is engaged to cement the modification of the original model of the world. Metaphor, whether used verbally or enacted, enormously expands the resources of the therapist for expression and the resources of the client for reception. Metaphor makes the unfamiliar familiar by relating commonalities in the familiar experience to the corresponding sequences within the unfamiliar one. The connection is labeled as understanding.

See if you can identify the analogical identification process in yourself by associating two seemingly dissimilar components of an unusual metaphor. Rather than attempting to interpret the metaphor, simply passively observe and "see" what arises in your consciousness. If nothing surfaces, it may be because most individuals are inexperienced at observing this capacity within. Here is the metaphor: "Santa Claus is as stubborn as a mule."

What happened inside when you understood Santa Claus

analogically to mulish stubbornness? Perhaps you experienced some uneasiness or minor disorientation. Then, you may have experienced a series of images associated with the overexposed cliché of the stubborn mule. You might have imagined a mule sitting on its hind legs while its owner struggled to get the mule to its feet. You may have noticed the owner had a great deal of exasperation and very little success to show for his efforts. In contrast, you may have had several images of Santa Claus, also overlearned. You may have seen a jolly, plump individual with his belly of jelly who offered his famous "Ho, ho, ho!" Then you may have observed an understanding of Santa Claus that formed in the context of stubbornness. Mulish aspects of Santa Claus may have appeared in your train of thought. It is possible to understand Santa Claus in a different way than before the association between Santa Claus and a mule arose. You may become aware of Santa Claus stubbornly resisting the foulest of weather to bring toys to children at Christmas. You may notice Santa Claus rigidly maintains the same beard and clothing year after year. You may even become aware of Santa Claus stubbornly refusing to relocate from the North Pole even though the climate is more inviting almost anywhere else in the world.

The point is, it is all but impossible to understand Santa Claus identically to the way one did before the associations between Santa Claus, the mule, and stubbornness were offered. It is as though a new facet has been added to the concept of Santa Claus that indelibly changes the previous understanding. In asking workshop participants to let themselves make associations to this metaphor, some have reported an additional change. For some the concept of stubbornness takes on a more positive connotation than before it was associated with Santa Claus. Stubbornness in the context of mule is different than in the context of Santa Claus. Placing the two in juxtaposition may modify both. Whether one's concept of Santa Claus or stubbornness or both are altered, the point remains that analogical connections do modify one's conceptualizations.

Notice that, initially, you were not told *what* the specific connections were between Santa Claus and the mule, only that these existed. You discovered (created) the associations yourself. In therapeutic metaphors the client discovers his own ideas rather than has them handed over by the therapist. Because the client demonstrates the relationship to himself through his own efforts, there can be more "pride in ownership." Understanding appears to come first to the right hemisphere of the client. Once the second-order change occurs, the client and therapist can work together to encode the new understanding left hemispherically (logically, verbally, etc.) as well. Registration in both hemispheres is thought to increase retention and the likelihood of change in behavior as well.

The ongoing processes associated with the right hemisphere will find a relationship, a connection between apparently disparate elements unless impeded by the left hemisphere critic ("Santa Claus isn't like a mule," "This is dumb"). In the Santa example, the new association adds another facet to understanding Santa Claus that modifies the concept. You likely had not understood stubbornness as a component of Santa's personality, but you are more likely to now.

The relationship-finding power of metaphor can be used to help the therapist form a conceptualization of the client's difficulties from all the bits and pieces of data offered by the client during assessment. The ability of metaphor to understand the unfamiliar in terms of the familiar can also be tapped to aid the client in reconceptualization during the intervention process.

A Method for Creating Therapeutic Metaphors

In order to create therapeutic metaphors, one can adopt a technique used by writers to overcome blocks called "clustering" (Rico, 1983, pp. 28-49). In clustering, a nucleus word or short phrase acts as a stimulus for recording associations that spring to mind. The associations are options from which the most appropriate find their way into the finished product. The associations are not forced, directed, or logically associated; rather, there is an "unthinking" quality to them akin to the spontaneous and uncommon associations that sometimes occur during dreaming. The associations are products of the thinking processes associated with the right hemisphere and are only impeded by intervention of the critiquing thinking processes associated with the left hemisphere. One lets the associations happen rather than makes them occur. The fact that there is no right or wrong way to cluster is precisely what can help practitioners overcome conceptual blocking not only in writing, but also in psychological assessment and intervention.

Therapeutic Metaphor in Assessment

All therapists occasionally experience difficulty in conceptualizing a client's difficulties. From the wealth of background history, client observations, client verbalizations, and other sources, one sometimes get a "feel" for what may be maintaining the symptoms, but cannot quite put it in words. Like a picture that is out of focus, areas of contour and contrast are discriminated, but not enough to identify specifics which remain obscure and blurred. This experience may be understood as one's left hemisphere struggling to verbally conceptualize patterns or relationships already registered in the right hemisphere.

Such was the case in the work with Annie, an intelligent and attractive individual who nonetheless suffered from severe depression. The onset of the depression coincided with her moving to a new location, although the move was planned and strongly desired by both her and her husband. Despite sleeplessness and appetite loss, fears of loss of control, and concentration difficulties, her primary concern was "not being able to be there for my child and my husband." Additional evidence suggested a biochemical component to her depression. Unfortunately, even after chemotherapy was begun, sustained improvement did not follow. Her husband believed her depression to be related to unresolved anger toward her father who had run his house in much the same way he managed his corporation. Autocratic orders and verbal dressing-downs were commonplace for both her and her mother who were relegated to roles of submissiveness and acquiescence. However, Annie had done well once separated from her father's influence during college. At this time, she felt most free, independent, and confident. Only when she married did she encounter depression, and the condition worsened when the couple moved.

The marriage was stable, with occasional struggles for control and use of passive-aggressive maneuvers. Within the therapy relationship, she proved to be compassionate and empathetic to the point of apology. When confronted with this, she related she was respectful of the therapist's "authority."

A "feel" for her predicament was achieved, but the conceptualization remained unsatisfyingly incomplete. To get an additional impression her therapist wrote "Annie is like . . ." and completed the phrase with any thoughts that came to mind. Here is the product:

Annie is like . . .

a pet that's been dominated by its owner.

a sailboat pushed along by any force that faces it.

a spool of thread.

The initial two associations were quickly and easily related to her early subjection and resulting submissiveness. The third appeared mysterious. When attempts to relate it to Annie's condition proved unsatisfying, associations to a spool of thread were written as well. The impressions of "unwinding" and "used to hold together things of beauty almost imperceptively" were hardly out before a hypothesis congealed that put all the data into place: Annie holds her marriage together by becoming unraveled herself. Subsequent sessions confirmed that she kept the peace in her marriage by the same appeasing strategy her mother successfully employed with her father. The more she relinquished control of her interests for the stability of the marriage, the more out of control she felt. Her husband, while responsive, appeared to draw strength from his dominance and consequently had difficulty appreciating the need to more consistently place her interests on equal footing with his own. The move appeared to culminate this gradual process of increasing selflessness. With this conceptualization in place, progress in therapy came quickly. Couple therapy was initiated to redefine the marriage and individual therapy concentrated on Annie's preserving control of herself within relationships. The depression lifted, she returned to her work, felt more spontaneous, and like "one of the gang again" with her friends. Occasional return episodes of depression appeared related to tensions within the marital relationship.

As in an embedded-figure puzzle where the ambiguity cre-

ated by a number of contiguous objects makes identification of
the targeted figure difficult, the presentation of a host of equally
weighted client-reported data poses a number of obstacles to
correct conceptualization. Once the correct context is discovered, however, it becomes nearly impossible not to see the correct juxtapositions from that point on. When the pattern in the
life of Annie was recognized and presented to her, she and her
therapist could see it nearly everywhere in her life. This metaphor-making strategy can become one technique among many
in any therapist's assessment arsenal.

Take the next 15 to 20 minutes and give yourself an opportunity to use the organizing, pattern-finding expertise of your
right hemisphere thinking processes to attempt to increase your
understanding of a client whose problem conceptualization has
proved elusive. For initial attempts you might find the following
steps useful.

1. Arrange for your time to be uninterrupted and without
other demands upon your resources. All you need is paper and
pen in front of you. For a few minutes suspend the influence of
your left hemisphere. When an association is formed for you by
your right hemisphere, avoid analyzing or criticizing the quality
or appropriateness of it. There are no right or wrong answers,
no logic or rules to follow. Impracticality is perfectly acceptable,
as is ambiguity. If you need to review the chapter on mental routines to become more receptive to analog thinking, please do so
before beginning.

2. Picture your client before you. Perhaps you will arrange
to have him seen in a characteristic pose or facial expression. Do
not interpret, censor, or edit these expressions; rather, simply
observe them. In a few moments you will begin associating.
Trust yourself. Let associations come up. Assume you will have
something come to mind that is relevant in some way. Begin
writing. Come up with three to five associations. Take as much
time as you need, but do not try too hard.

3. Now that you have finished your associations, use both
hemispheres to relate them more fully to your client and to test
for "fit." For the ones that are readily related to your client's difficulties, add the word "because" and finish the statement with
as many specific examples as you would like until you feel it is

verified. For example, Annie's therapist could have said she is like a sailboat pushed along by the breeze because she derives her strength from what others are willing to give her rather than from within. Specifically, she is like a sailboat pushed along by the breeze because she waited for her husband to take her car in to be fixed rather than do so herself, because she ate strawberries offered by her husband even though to do so would result in hives, and because she consented to go to a party she did not want to attend.

As you add specifics, did you find they came easily and confirm your association (even though you might add to it or otherwise modify it) or do you experience them as forced or contrived? In the statements above relating Annie to a sailboat, many of her experiences appeared to fit well. The elaborations suggested she would profit from less dependency and greater self-reliance to restabilize her marriage. The associations were useful. If your reality check proved too stilted, the association in its present form may not be usable. Can it be modified to tease, from the association, the relevance your intuition indentified with your client? If not, simply lay it aside.

4. If there are associations that came to you but appear puzzling (like the "spool of thread" example), shift into your pattern-finding mode again and continue to associate. Do not attempt to confirm the reality of the associations for now (i.e., avoid adding the "because" clause).

5. Now, take the second-order associations and see how well they fit the evidence you have about your client as you did previously with first-order associations. Use the "because" test for "fit."

6. In doing so, did you stimulate your thinking about your client? Were you able to reorganize your interpretation of him? Does the reorganization satisfy the data you have accumulated better than previous hypotheses?

If this metaphor-making exercise was not immediately helpful to you, do not give up or lose faith in it. Some individuals find this metaphor-making method more accessible than others. With practice most will be able to tolerate, if not actually enjoy, the temporary chaos of pattern genesis without feeling inhibited or silly. Nothing always works, and this will be no exception.

Therapeutic Metaphor in Intervention

The example of metaphor with the depressed physical therapist that opened the chapter demonstrates that therapeutic
metaphors can augment a therapeutic approach because of the
power they possess to facilitate reconceptualization. In addition,
use of metaphor can increase expressiveness of the therapist in a
way that creates a lasting impression on the client. Rice (1965)
reports a therapist's expressive vocal style and use of fresh, vivid
language significantly correlates with positive change whereas
"artificial" voice and jargon correlates with negative outcomes.
Another example will be used to illustrate.

Robin had been a bright, active child. He was well cared for
and loved by both his parents. They "gave him everything" in
order that he be able to make the most of his potential. They acknowledged they were "permissive," not wanting to inhibit his
unfolding development. They had little understanding that they
were permissive to the point of laxity and oversolicitiousness.
Because Robin received what he demanded he had little opportunity or need to learn to delay gratification, tolerate frustration,
or to curb impulsiveness. Why should he learn to cooperate
when he received what he wanted whether he cooperated or
not? The parents had minimized his condition by reassuring
themselves it was all "just a stage." As Robin became older, the
ramifications of his stages became greater. By the time his parents sought consultation during his adolescence (he would not
come in), Robin was abusive of them and others, had dropped
out of school, wrecked his car, and recently dropped any pre-
tense of not using drugs and alcohol continuously.

Robin appeared both drug addicted and strikingly ill-
equipped to deal with his dependence or the life stresses that he
had sheltered himself from with substances. Whatever he could
learn to do to better prepare himself for adult living would have
to follow treatment for his drug dependence in a residential facility. He clearly would not enter voluntarily and his parents
had carried respect for his privacy and self-direction to such extremes that they could not initiate the referral against his wishes.
It appeared important to leave his parents with vivid images of
the family's condition that could not be ignored or easily mini-

mized. It was hoped that by doing so chances would be greater that they would actively intervene despite Robin's anticipated stinging protests. An appropriate approach appeared to be one that educated them about drug addiction, painted a realistically bleak picture of their son's short future if they did not intervene, and referral to a rehabilitation facility. Metaphors could be sought through clustering to undermine a continuation of their faulty conceptualization of parental caring.

Take the stimulus phrase "respecting privacy is good, but not interfering to a fault is like . . ." and open yourself to the association-finding ability of the right hemisphere in order to give images of the same form. If you would like, pause a few minutes and write associations that spring to mind for you. Here are some possibilities:

> stagnant water
>
> obesity
>
> Kitty Genovese being stabbed to death while neighbors watched
>
> not voting at elections
>
> not watering plants

Each of these offer promise of vivid, yet unconventional images which emphasize their difficulty to the parents, influencing them to modify their confusion of caring and unwillingness to interfere:

One could acknowledge with them that their permissive approach to parenting has been one of not making waves in their relationship with their son. This opening could be followed by asking them if they know what one gets by literally not making waves. After some effort has been expended and if they did not arrive at the correct answer, the therapist could inform them that stagnant water is the product of not making waves. Is this the way they want to characterize their relationship with their son? If not, what are they willing to do?

They could be asked to agree that some eating is good. Then, they could be asked whether if some eating is good, obesity is better? After they explain that too much of a good thing does not make it better, their wisdom could be applied to their predicament.

They could be asked if they have heard the true story of Kitty Genovese. If not; the therapist could explain to them that she was the young woman stabbed many times over the course of a half hour until she died while 38 of her neighbors looked from their windows. They could be further asked what feelings they experience as they hear about this incident of bystander apathy. The therapist could then suggest that these will be the feelings with which they will have to live if their son dies without their intervention. They could be further asked what they thought Kitty Genovese would have liked done for her by her neighbors. Would they be willing to do the same for their son?

They could be asked if they believe in democracy. When they answer in the affirmative, the therapist could ask them why people should vote, being sure to solicit several reasons. Then he could say, "But wouldn't voting be interfering with the election process?" In this manner they could be helped to bridge the gap between participation and responsibility on the one hand and intrusiveness and irresponsibility on the other.

Finally, the therapist could ask them to buy a small plant that looks healthy at the time of purchase and place it by a sunny window that they are sure to pass daily. However, they are not to interfere with its growth by watering it until their son is placed in a drug rehabilitation center.

These metaphors, judiciously used and strategically woven into the fabric of the total consultation, are thought to increase the probability of retention of the material to which they are related analogically. They are unexpected, even novel, ways to amplify the discussion that not only interrupt the assimiliation process of the left hemisphere, but also suggest a way to take the theme of the session home for daily viewing. Look at the list of associations you derived from the stimulus statement. Play with them. Elaborate upon them in a way that is as impactive as possible. What ideas do you have for implementing them that maximizes acceptance and minimizes rejection?

An artificial learning formula will be summarized that can be used to practice making metaphors for psychotherapeutic interventions until the practice becomes a naturally occurring phenomenon during the course of therapy sessions.

1. Begin by stating the therapeutic issue or client misconception that inhibits symptom alleviation or securing more desirable outcomes. This may take something of the form of "The problem with the client is. . . ."

2. Deemphasize your critical and critiquing left hemisphere as before. Remind yourself that you can be as nonsensical as you need to be to produce associations. There are no right or wrong ones.

3. Now you are ready to begin by simply adding "like" to the stimulus phrase so you have the format "The problem with this client is like . . ." and letting the associations arise. Let them keep coming until you have several.

4. Afterwards, use the expertise of your left hemisphere processing to embellish and polish your creations for greater impact. Can you relate the metaphor to areas or experiences with which the client is already familiar (e.g., vocation, hobbies, sports, music) in order to maximize using the familiar to discover a more realistic, albeit unfamiliar, interpretation of experience? Does your language style enhance expressiveness by using words geared for sensory impact? How can you make each metaphor more humorous, entertaining, or otherwise evocative in order to enhance retention? There is no correct or incorrect metaphor. Each is to be judged solely upon its utility.

5. Finally, how can you present the ramifications of your metaphor in question format that will help your client get the most from your metaphor? Statements made in response to questions engage the client's left hemisphere in confirming the new conceptualization by relating it to specific experiences in the client's life.

The more this metaphor-making strategy is practiced, the more proficient one becomes at making and using analogical connections with clients and the more internalized the process will become for the individual. In a manner similar to that of a beginner teaching himself to ride a bicycle, these "training wheel" steps can be set aside as confidence and mastery grows. In time, analogy-making can become like second nature in many crucial therapeutic circumstances.

A POTPOURRI OF THERAPEUTIC APPLICATIONS

Motivating for Psychotherapy

Rabkin (1977, pp. 18-25) aptly reports that clients enter therapy not just with symptoms, but also feeling demoralized about their ability to do something about their symptoms. In many ways, clients can be unfamiliar with or at least out of touch with their past successes and their reasonable hope for success in therapy. Clients may be distrustful of their resources, efforts, and ability to evoke change in themselves. Metaphor may be used to rekindle hope, motivate behavioral change, structure therapy, and reacquaint clients with prior successes. Here are a few examples, among many, of possible therapist statements to clients that use metaphor to address motivational issues. All share in common the making of analogical connections between an experience with which the client is already familiar and a pertinent therapeutic issue of the same form:

"Have you ever noticed that people you see diving off a high diving platform appear to be having fun doing so? Do you think it started out as fun for them? How do you account for the change? That's right, what initially is frightening can actually become fun with effort and practice. Can you see how dating (school, self-reliance, making conversation) can become that way for you? Where are you willing to start?"

"Improvement in therapy can be kind of like planting corn. Much effort at first shows little results, but can bring about a great harvest in the long run." (Contributed by Steve Young)

"Are you familiar with the principle of inertia? Have you ever had the experience of trying to push a car (or anything heavy on wheels)? It's hard to get started, but once you get going it is even more difficult to stop. That's the way self-improvement can be. It requires a great deal of energy at first just to get rolling, but, in time, becomes so rewarding you don't want to return to old ways of being."

"Remember how it was when you first learned to drive a car (tie your shoelaces, write your name)? That's right, it took a great deal of concentrated effort. And even with that you made plenty of mistakes and felt awfully awkward as you saw many people do easily the very thing you struggled with. How forced or difficult is it to drive a car now? It's almost like second nature. What once was difficult is a part of you now. What makes you think becoming assertive (holding a job, etc.) will be any different?"

"Remember a time when you adopted a new style of clothing (or hairstyle). Can you remember how you felt quite awkward and self-conscious at first, but as you acclimated to the new clothes they actually became your favorites? The same kind of thing can happen when trying on new behaviors as well."

"If you were to teach someone to swim, would you throw them into the deep end or begin in the shallow part of the pool? That's right, you don't start out in the deep end even if you eventually want to be able to swim there because it would be overwhelming at first. I'm hoping our work together will be as nurturing as your approach to your swimmer—and with similar long range results."

"Do you have a savings account? Why? That's right, in order to plan for the future you put money into your savings now. You know that the more you put into it now the more you will eventually get out of it. Therapy can be an investment in your future as well."

Feeling Worse in Order to Get Better

Many clients with unsuccessful problem-solving strategies have little faith that temporary discomfort can lead to long-lasting reward. Typically, their strategies have resulted in the small discomfort becoming even greater. The inhibiting effect compromises their taking an active-initiative role in their therapy. Reminders from their own experience that the experience of some pain can lead to eventual pain reduction can be reassuring. Here is a sample:

"Have you had the experience of a toothache and, even knowing you needed to see a dentist, you didn't want to go? What motivated you to finally go? Right, to end the pain. But it would hurt to have the cavity filled. Why go through the discomfort? You were willing to go through greater pain now in order to end the pain or increase your comfort in the future. And you'll be spending most of your time in the future! You've told me about your parents "nagging" you to find work and about your desire for a car, both of which are a source of discomfort. Can you make a connection between the dental experience and your inclination to settle for the security of a dependent relationship with your parents rather than to begin working to get what you want? Will it become harder to find work and begin working the longer you put it off? Will you do it some day anyway? Would you tell someone with a toothache to put off going to the dentist until the pain becomes intolerable, knowing that the drilling will be deeper and hurt more than if they went at the first sign of a problem? If you can see it with a toothache, then see it with yourself and employment."

"Have you ever had a favorite pair of shoes that you were to used to and enjoyed so much you didn't want to trade them in for a new pair? Did you hold on to them to the point that they were beyond repair and a new pair became a necessity? Remember how awkward and stiff that new pair was compared to the custom fit of the older pair? What eventually happened with the new pair? Yes, they became as comfortable as the older pair, but far more supportive and even more in style. Do you think the same thing could be true about trying on more up-to-date behavior?"

"Have you ever taught yourself a skill like tennis or typing and then received instruction from a professional? Did you discover that at first you played worse or typed slower as you readjusted, but, because you stuck with it, you far outperformed your previous level? I believe this is the kind of satisfaction you'll have if you stick with the short-term frustration of changing some of your strategies that are good, but not good enough for you to settle for."

Dealing with Impulses

For individuals who have not learned to optimally express and implement impulses, their own urges can become tyrannical and punitive. The result frequently is estrangement from oneself. Impulses can become overcontrolled to the extent that few are acted upon or, at the other extreme, so undercontrolled that nearly all are acted upon because one "felt" like it. Following are two examples of metaphors that have proven effective in reconceptualizing overcontrol and undercontrol issues, respectively:

"Do you believe fire to be potentially beneficial? Yes, it's useful as a source of fuel, heat, and light. But it can become harmful. If you strike a match and burn your finger in doing so, should you never use fire again or should you learn to manage it to get the full benefits of it? If you can see it with fire, can you see it with your sexual behavior (anger, etc.)?"

"I'd like to talk with you about something that may relate to your overeating (substance abuse, returning to abusive relationships, overspending, etc.). Have you ever wondered how parents teach their children to be spoiled brats? Let's assume we have a mother and son. When the child wants something the mother gives it to him whether it's good for the child or not. As a result he has difficulty coming to know what is or isn't good for him. And if the mother tries to be helpful by refusing, the child throws a tantrum until she gives in.

"What has the mother taught her son? Right, he has learned if he pitches a fit long enough and loud enough, he'll eventually get what's desired, whether it's good for him or not. Suppose the mother comes to recognize the self-defeating nature of this interaction and decides to stop teaching the boy that throwing a tantrum or whining is an effective means to get what one wants from others. What do you predict will happen when she first refuses the child's inappropriate demands? Right! The son will think, 'All I have to do is yell long enough and loud enough and I'll eventually get what I want whether it's good for me or not.' If the child keeps it up a long time and the parent finally does give in, that would be confirming the child's prediction. What would you expect to transpire the next time he wants something his mother doesn't want him to have and his mother decided to put an end to the tantrum behavior? Yes, he would redouble his efforts to compel her to give in since it worked so well before. If the mother remained resolved not to give in no matter how long or how hard the tantrum because she has her child's best interests at heart, what do you expect would eventually happen?

"Exactly, if the mother does not give in, at first the child's behavior will be worse. This will be a sign that she is on the right track. Eventually, he will recognize that no matter how great the tantrum, the strategy is ineffective. The tantrums will diminish in intensity and eventually fade away. There may be intermittent explosions to test his mother's resolve, but if she remains resolute, the whininess will be at such low intensity and so occasional that it becomes easy to manage.

"I think you may have taught your body to throw a tantrum at the slightest urge to eat. What do you think? What do you want to do about it? What do you expect will happen if you don't give in to the urge except when it's actually time to eat?"

Marital Issues

Metaphor can be particularly effective in marital and family therapies by serving as a common denominator between all the diverse conceptualizations of the members of the system. As such, metaphors can help bridge the gaps caused by differing early learning histories of spouses and the limited experience of the children. Satir has been described as being particularly effective at translating one family member's experience into a medium readily understood by another (Bandler & Grinder, 1979, pp. 40-42). Satir appears to be gifted at using one member's representation of experience as a metaphor for interpreting the actions of another family member.

For example, a husband may measure satisfaction kinesthetically through physical comfort. His wife, on the other hand, may measure satisfaction visually by what "looks good." She may interpret his scattering things around to be comfortable as disrespectful to her. He may interpret her having everything neat as leaving little "elbow room" for him to be comfortable. Each feels misunderstood, but neither knows why. In an example like this, Satir explained to the husband the way he would feel if he got into a bed with cracker crumbs (kinesthetic discomfort) is the way his wife feels when she walks into a room with his stuff scattered about (visual discomfort). By making the analogical link, she teaches greater empathy.

An experience familiar to one family member can be used to achieve a greater appreciation of another. Consider the example of a workaholic husband and his wife who referred themselves for marital therapy because his dedication to work ("Without me working as much as I do to earn the money I do, Sally wouldn't have all the nice things she does. I don't understand why she's so upset that I put work first") and insufficient consideration ("I know I don't call her when I'm going to work late, but I don't want to take the time out to call") had contributed to her feeling devalued and estranged from him. Earlier he had two brief "one-night stands" that were attractive precisely for their ability to decrease tensions without emotional involvement, consideration, or commitment. In a let's-level-with-each-other session he revealed to his wife the two affairs. Because he characteristically separated his feelings from his actions, he appeared genuinely puzzled that she would react so strongly ("I try to be honest with her and now she's less trusting than ever"). As the implication of his statement was "Honesty works against a stable marriage," an analogy was made using his business sense to increase his empathy for his wife:

"Suppose your bookkeeper, who had been with the firm for many years, told you he had been embezzling. Would you be so quick to trust him with your money again? Why not, he leveled with you?"

By using the highly familiar venue of the workplace, he grasped an understanding that an implicit breach of trust is not quickly healed either for him or his wife. Later in the same session, he wanted to minimize his wife's hurt by saying the affair should not matter to her since they were loveless one-night stands. The therapist borrowed from the earlier metaphor to keep him focused on the real issue of breach of trust within a relationship:

"What if the bookkeeper said the money went to a good cause. Would it matter to you?" The intervention effectively undermined his rationalization and helped him be accountable for the effects of his actions on his marriage.

Another frequently encountered example is that of one marital partner who does not tell the other what is wanted and then feels angry or uncared about when the partner does not know. Unfortunately, even if the partner asks what is the matter, he or she is rebuked under the rationale that if the partner cared sufficiently, he or she would know intuitively. A brief, effective metaphor uses a grocery store motif:

"Suppose you were in a grocery store and were interested in buying a can of peas. If you were interested in the cost and the can were unmarked, who would you go to see about it and why? Right, you'd ask someone who worked there because it is their store and they are in the best spot to know the price of any of the items. Suppose you asked the cashier and he said, 'Guess!' How would you feel? Now you know how your partner feels when you have him/her guess. Do you want him/her feeling that way? What can you do to get a different outcome?" (Based on a suggestion by Glen King.)

Couples can apply their shared experience with their children toward reinterpreting marital issues. For example, what parents have not had the experience of trying to get their children to eat something because it is good for them? Similarly, one partner may want the other "for his/her own good" to do something he/she is unwilling to do with predictable negative results. How can you construct a metaphor using the forced feeding experience to help bridge this marital gap? Please consider this before reading further. Did you help the couple understand that even if one forces compliance, the price paid may be resentment or an entrenched opposition leading to further "control" struggles? Did you ask them how else parents can increase the probability children will eat spinach, but without negative ploys ("Eat this now if you want a cookie later. It's up to you.") Finally, did you help them apply their findings to their marriage?

Metaphor can be useful to help an individual conceptualize choices associated with staying or leaving a relationship itself. These choices are particularly difficult as answers are rarely clear-cut and almost always are fraught with trade-offs and second-guessing. Without some framework, the difficult work can become even more of a struggle. Here are two of many possible analogies to relationships:

"The decision before you reminds me of a stockholder invested in a company that isn't doing well. Maybe we can use it to help bring into focus your choices with your relationship. Suppose you invest heavily in a stock you buy at $20 per share because it looks promising. Suppose, hwoever, it drops to $15 a share. Do you sell it to cut your losses or do you hope it has bottomed out and will rise again to its former level or even better? If you reason that because it looked promising at $20 it will likely improve rather than worsen at $15 a share, you might decide to hang with it a while. However, suppose it drops to $10 a share? If you sell now you lose more than you would have earlier, but you still recoup half of your investment. Can you see the dilemma? There is no right formula for when to hold on or to bail out. It's a personal decision with many unknowns and risks either way. I don't want you to feel misled that I can offer you something for either the stock market or marriage that will make a difficult decision a certain one. I can work with you to set criteria acceptable to you from which to base decisions. For example, with a stock you can set a price that should it fall below you will sell no matter what. Or you can set a value that if it falls there you will invest more heavily hoping for sharp improvement. Can you apply this line of thought to your marital choices in a way that salvages as much of your self-esteem as possible?"

"Your struggle to find a comfortable degree of closeness with your alcoholic husband is like the dilemma of a camper seeking the optimal distance from a campfire that dwindles in intensity as the fuel is used up. If the camper is too far away from the fire she feels too cold; but if she gets too close she gets burned. The camper can get a blanket to insulate herself against extremes of hot or cold, or build her own fire rather than rely upon an unreliable one. Can you see how these are like some of your options in your marriage? Are there other options for the camper? What is the counterpart to the camper's blanket for you in your marriage?"

CHAPTER 5

THERAPEUTIC EXTENSIONS
OF METAPHOR

Knowing anything in its deepest sense means knowing how
to be creative with it.

—Elliot Eisner

CONSTRUCTING METAPHOR-BASED INTERVENTIONS

The success of a therapeutic metaphor is contingent upon
having it packaged so as to have as much impact on the client as
possible. Factors that influence attention and retention as well
as those that dramatize the intervention can be manipulated
optimally by the therapist to facilitate client reconceptualization
of a faulty model of the world.

Methods to Secure Attention

Recall that individuals are neurologically predisposed to be
selectively attentive. A stimulus has a greater likelihood of being
detected if it moves, changes, or otherwise contrasts from pre-
ceding and surrounding stimuli. The following are specific types
of "attention grabbers."

Orienting stimuli.   The next time you view television, notice how advertisers introduce their announcements. Each ad-
vertisement begins with sounds (whistle or horn, dog bark,
sneezes, etc.), phrases ("Look!" "Oh no!" "Hi there!" etc.), or
provocative questions ("Does your house have roaches?") designed to orient the viewer to the television screen. Therapists
can use these and other orienting stimuli to gain the full attention of a client before presenting the strategically placed therapeutic metaphor.

Changes in voice tone, volume, or cadence are particularly
effective for verbal metaphor. Orators know the value of the
"pregnant pause" before presenting the key portion of their or-
atory, and therapists can follow their lead before presenting the
metaphor. A well-placed profanity or other exclamation can
punctuate the message for greater impact. Using the client's
name before key statements is perhaps the most commonly used
orienting stimulus by therapists and quite effective at securing
full attention.

Importantly, the metaphor-derived intervention itself,
while highly related to client material on a formal level, contrasts
sharply on a content level with client reports that precede it. For
example, the ambiguity created by introducing the subject of
grocery store checkout lines to the anxious physical therapist
who was describing employment problems (see previous chapter) provoked her curiosity to the extent that she became highly
alert.

A variety of nonverbal orienting stimuli can be offered to
clients as well. Strategically placed postural changes, pencil tapping, or even squeaking one's chair can be orienting for a client.

Unusual juxtaposition.   The unexpected captures attention. Novel stimuli in familiar surroundings (e.g., a Chinese restaurant in the midst of a row of hamburger stands) and familiar
stimuli in novel surroundings (e.g., a McDonald's restaurant in
downtown Hong Kong) immediately catch one's eye. Analogical
connections *are*, of course, unusual juxtapositions in themselves.
Fresh, meaningful associations offered to the client in therapy
are akin to the powerful metaphors of memorable literature that
provide lasting impressions for generations. For example, to
associate the accident proneness for which a client has sought
treatment with psychogenic impotence may appear unusual, if

not startling, to the client. If the client is accepting of the interpretation of impotence as performance anxiety, this can become the basis for understanding performance anxiety in the familiar, yet poorly understood, accident proneness of the sufferer.

Engagement.   Individuals are more likely to attend to that in which they are actively involved than to something in which they are passive recipients. Passengers in a car, for example, are usually less vigilant to traffic and road conditions than the driver, even though both are travelers. Therapeutic interventions that engage the client's senses, intellect, and behavior are thought to have a greater likelihood of registration than those that do not. Consider the appeal to the client's senses in the following metaphor that likens a group therapy participant's awakening potential to a sparkler:

"When I heard you talk just now about calling friends you've been out of touch with and taking swimming lessons at the "Y," I had the strongest image of you as a big, bright sparkler bursting into flame. Sparks are flying off everywhere and I can almost feel the heat! It's like the Fourth of July. Come to think of it, isn't your trying out new activities kind of like your personal Independence Day?"

One traditional way therapists have engaged the intellect of clients is by asking questions, especially open-ended ones that require more than a "yes" or "no" response. Metaphorical communication has a built-in capacity for intellectual engagement. In order to translate the analogical associations into logical ones, clients actively recode the input from impressionistic to verbal symbolization.

Enactment of a metaphor, rather than simply articulating it, may also heighten the experience for clients. Some of the interventions that follow exemplify activity in metaphorical communication.

What else grabs your attention? How can you apply this to any therapeutic communication?

Methods to Insure Retention

No sharp dividing line exists between attentional and retentional factors. Because adequate attention is prerequisite to memorizing, what aids in attention supports retention as well.

Nonetheless, the following are additional influences of retention.

Meaningfulness.   Few readers would be surprised to learn that an individual is more apt to remember something meaningful than something nonsensical. For example, research has consistently supported that words are more easily learned and recalled than nonsense syllables. Of course, metaphors that carry much relevance to the reality issues they seek to illuminate are desired in therapy as well. To the extent they "sound like Greek" to a client, the therapist is relating the unfamiliar with the unfamiliar. To do so may provoke curiosity in some, but for most it is more likely to result in little reconceptualization and possibly even greater demoralization. For example, comparing ineffectual parental limit-setting to inaccurate mitre cuts in framemaking may be apt, but carries little relevance for an individual unfamiliar with woodworking. With the association obscured, the metaphor is useless or even destructive.

Entertainment.   Enjoyment has a way of maintaining attention and stimulating recall that far outweighs the strongest exhortation. Material presented in a "catchy," humorous, or interesting manner stands out from mundane expression of similar themes. Fresh, novel presentations done with a "flair for the dramatic" can make for memorable performances even within the therapeutic hour. Consider this example by psychologist Tom Kuhlman, as reported in *Reader's Digest* (October 1984, p.49):

> A patient gave her doctor such a steady dirge of bad things happening to her that one day he wore a black arm-band to reflect her attitude. She burst out laughing: it was a watershed in their doctor-patient relationship.

The unexpected.   Dr. Kuhlman stepped outside the traditional bounds of expected verbal therapy by enacting humorously his reaction to the client's attitude. The results were highly successful. Most clients expect kindness and respect from their therapists; their current faulty worldviews frequently absorb many expressions of compassion, attentiveness, and caring without significant modification. When sufficient rapport is achieved, the therapist has the opportunity to model greater spontaneity and flexibility without jeopardizing the relationship or discouraging (or possibly frightening) the client. Operating outside the expected therapist role, as Dr. Kuhlman did, created an unexpected, vivid, and entertaining picture of the impact the client had on others that is unforgettable.

Simplification and exaggeration. Paradoxically, clarity can be enhanced at times by stretching a phenomenon out of proportion. Consider this example of metaphorical simplification by a colleague to help a young couple decide if they are ready to raise children. Each was asked to carry a raw egg everywhere for 1 week before meeting once again with the therapist. At that time the therapist asked if the eggs were intact and inquired as to the degree of burden attached to carrying for the safety of the eggs. In doing so, he helped the couple reach conclusions about children. The egg metaphor greatly simplified the demands of child rearing while also bringing into sharp relief for the couple their degree of preparedness for the demands of caring for a highly dependent infant.

An example of exaggeration makes use of a common story vehicle in soap operas. A conflicted couple reported great love for one another as well as substantial distrust. Observations of the couple's interactions suggested that each tended to omit pertinent facts that might hurt or worry the other. For example, the husband would not tell his wife they were nearly overdrawn at the bank because she would worry; yet she would become unnerved at his mounting anxiety and frequently would misinterpret it. When she discovered the state of their finances anyway, she felt demeaned by him and wondered what else was being kept from her. At the same time, however, she would not inform him of their children's poor grades in school so as to shelter him from additional distress. When the principal sent a note home to be signed by both parents the husband felt annoyed and skeptical of his wife's motives for excluding him.

Each was assigned the task of watching at least two soap operas for a week. They were to look for occasions where lovers did not tell the truth to the partner because they did not want to hurt one another. They were asked to take special notice of what happened to the relationship as a result. Each observed that misleading one's lover, even if motivated by love, was highly destructive. Even if the couple's misguided protectiveness was motivated by factors aside from the reported ones, exposure to the exaggeration of the phenomenon in soap operas forever blemished the innocence with which it was once done.

Incompletion.   Zeigarnik (1927) presented subjects with a series of different tasks, half of which were interrupted before completion and half of which were not. Immediately afterward, the subjects were asked to name as many of the tasks as they could recall. Interestingly, only 8 percent of the subjects recalled completed and incompleted tasks equally well. Eighty percent remembered more unfinished tasks than completed ones, and the remaining 12 percent remembered more of the completed ones. It appears that unfinished business often increases retention. This "Zeigarnik effect" can be applied to interventions using therapeutic metaphors. For example, a therapist can present an unelaborated metaphor in one session and ask the client to consider how the metaphor applies to the reality issues of the client during the interval between sessions. Similarly, the client can be offered an ambiguous assignment with only the comment that "There is something in this that will be useful to you." The client is implicitly challenged to complete the assignment and relate it to his goals without having to be directed to do so. Given the context of a helping relationship, the client is likely to interpret the metaphor or assignment in a growth-facilitating manner. It is thought that individuals are apt to learn best and value more that which they have derived from their own efforts as opposed to information simply given to them.

Repetition and uniqueness.   Individuals are more likely to remember something distinctive (yet meaningful) as well as something to which they have been repeatedly exposed (unless to the point of saturation). Use of multiple metaphors indentical in theme for a particular issue is a means of resolving the apparent paradox of maintaining distinctiveness while also repeating exposures. In the example of the distraught parents of the teenage addict from the previous chapter, metaphors that discriminate healthy involvement in the welfare of the son from intrusiveness into his privacy were offered in a variety of ways. Therapist-generated metaphors are uncommon ways of intervening that offer contrast from input of others. Their number can be as great as a therapist's experience is broad and concept-making ability is flexible.

The interventions described below are designed to illustrate use of metaphor and right hemisphere processing in reconcep-tualization and behavioral change. All are geared to engage the client as fully as possible.

METAPHOR-DERIVED INTERVENTIONS

Therapeutic Experiments

The experience of a phenomenon is far more compelling than simply talking about it. Metaphorically derived experiments share in common with all experimentation the performance of a sequence of actions in order to learn from the outcome. The actions are closely related to the reality issues presented, but at an analogical level. For example, the couple who carried an egg for a week were given the experience of the demands of parenting without actually becoming a parent. Because of the analogical connection they were able more clearly to conceptualize their readiness for parenting and reach a decision about parenting at that time.

Glen King (personal communication, 1983) has developed an analogical approach to help clients struggling with issues of giving and taking in caring relationships. The following enact-ment of his approach enlightens an individual who has given away too much of herself in relationships and then complains of abandonment:

Therapist: Imagine you and I meet and come to know each other. Imagine this pillow [therapist hands her a pillow] I'm giving you represents all the loyalty, faithfulness, love, car-ing, concern, sexuality, and so on you have to offer. Sup-pose at one point in the relationship I say to you, "What you have there is very interesting. I'd like to have it. Give it to me." [Therapist takes her pillow from her lap.] How are you feeling now?

Client: A little empty.

Therapist: I've got it all and you've got none.

Client [gesturing to pillow in therapist's lap]: I want your pillow.

Therapist: What will you do for it?

Client: I gave you mine; now give me yours.

Therapist: You gave it away. I've got it all. Why should I work hard to give you anything back? [Pause] Does it make you feel played with?

Client: Definitely!

Therapist: The nice thing about my position is that I've got so much that I can go trade with someone else and because you're so empty you're going to need to hang on to get it back. [Pause] The guy's got all the goodies and you've got an empty feeling. Is this what has occurred before?

Client: That's what has happened. But not any more. I'm not going to get involved anymore.

Therapist: Right. If it happens to you several times, then what happens one time when a guy comes up and says, "Give me your pillow?"

Client [emphatically]: No way!

Therapist: If you're not going to be giving some of yourself, why should I stick around? [Pause] How's that sounding to you?

Client: Awfully lonely.

Therapist: And loneliness isn't what you're after. You want respectful treatment in a relationship. So tell me, what do I have to do to get some of your caring and so on to begin a relationship? What can we work out?

Client: Give me yours first.

Therapist: If I do that then I run the risk of being in the position you've been in. What can we work out that's fair?

Client: You give me some of your pillow and I'll give you some of mine.

Therapist: Hold it. There's a danger in that for me. You'll have just as much as when you started. What am I going to have to do to hold on to you?

Client: Treat me right!

In this way, the therapist helps the client to develop relationships slowly to establish a foundation of reciprocity, of trading and negotiating in a sharing partnership.

Many of the games and puzzles used as illustrations in this book can be used effectively with clients as analogical experiences to be enacted and from which generalizations can be applied to reality issues. The entrapped Ping-Pong ball puzzle can introduce a client to his constricted problem-solving ability due to self-imposed taboos. The OTTFFSS puzzle vividly demonstrates how reading complexity into problems that do not require it can impede solution finding. The nine-dot puzzle illustrates how failures in solutions can be attributed to the faulty definition of the problem by the individual. The specific contents of the problems in living vary greatly among clients who resemble one another closely on these meta-levels.

A commonly encountered client phenomenon is that of having difficulty accepting that expectations derived from prior experiences can influence one's interpretation of current experience. Winning the client's belief in transference is such an example. Many clients prefer to believe that situations cause their reactions rather than that their expectations influence the interpretation of the situation. A simple yet persuasive demonstration of the influence of prior experience on present perception can be accomplished by using sets of drawings originally published by Bugelski (1964, p. 179). These are reproduced in Figure 5.1. The client is shown the row of heads and asked to name the sex of each figure. Next, the client is shown the row of animals and asked to identify the type of animal. Invariably, the last drawing is described as a man when shown in the context of other humans and as a rodent when shown following an exposure to other animals, despite their being identical drawings. Little effort is usually required for the client to apply experience with the demonstration to learning history.

Another experiment takes advantage of the client as his own analog. An otherwise competent young woman was self-conscious to the extent that her interpersonal life suffered greatly. As an elementary school teacher she performed her role ably and spontaneously. In the company of adults, however, she inhibited herself by anticipating her remarks and actions to be embarrassing to herself, hurtful to others, or otherwise worthy of negative evaluation. To dramatize her ability to create discomfort by overly scrutinizing herself, she was asked to become aware of the sensation of her belt around her waist and the pres-

Figure 5.1. Demonstration of how expectation shapes perception. Used with permission of Macmillan Publishing Company from *The Psychology of Learning Applied to Teaching* (Revised Edition) by B. R. Bugelski. Copyright © 1964, 1971 by Macmillan Publishing Company.

sure of her shoes on her feet. By shifting awareness to these areas she came in touch with discomfort in areas where previously there was none. Once she redirected her attention outward, the discomfort vanished. Her discovery was applied to her self-consciousness. Rather than increase self-scrutiny to decrease self-consciousness (as she had been practicing), she became sensitized to the importance of selective inattention to some of her thoughts in order not to compromise her spontaneity.

Another possibility takes advantage of the clinic experience itself as an analog to other real life situations. Steve had begun therapy in a depressed state that appeared strongly associated to his unassertiveness. He applied himself to this therapy, learning assertive principles and performing well during behavioral rehearsal in the therapy hour. Therefore, the next session was intentionally begun 15 minutes late. His therapist accepted complete responsibility for the late start and apologized for his tardiness. At the end of the 45-minute session, he was given a charge slip marked for 1 hour to take to the billing clerk. In checking with her later, she informed the therapist that he had brought the "error" to her attention quite appropriately. At the next meeting, Steve and his therapist discussed how his ability to deal with the 5 minutes of anxiety he experienced to draw her attention to the inaccuracy resulted in hours of feeling good about himself because he took care of his interests.

Metaphorical Homework

Therapeutic homework is a tradition in many therapies because assignments identify the client as an active participant in the therapy and stretch the therapy throughout the entire interval between sessions. Metaphorical homework assignments are symbolic enactments to facilitate problem reconceptualization and resolution rather than direct attempts to build skills.

Traditional cultural rituals prescribe specific actions for individuals to perform on a metaphorical level to aid in healing or mark transitions. Burials, weddings, even high school graduations are cultural homages to what is being left behind and markings for new beginnings as well. Therapeutic rituals have been prescribed by many family therapists to help stymied families reorganize at stress points in the family cycle (e.g., Haley, 1973; Whitaker, 1975). Palazzoli, Boscolo, Cecchin, and Prata (1977) believe "the physical enactment of a ritual is infinitely more productive than any form of verbalization can hope to be" (p. 445). Fish (1973) has taken a step further. He asserts that "the theoretical and factual content of therapy doesn't matter; the treatment is the ritual of therapy itself, invested with faith and expectancy by both healer and sufferer." The interested reader is directed to a comprehensive handling of the subject by the Dutch psychologist, Onno van der Hart (1983). For illustration purposes, a brief example of a therapeutic ritual is excerpted from van der Hart and Ebbers (1981).

Mrs. Jansen had come to an outpatient clinic with complaints of instability, depression, fear of people, and loneliness. Her developmental history offered little precedent for stability, since it included a stay in an orphanage after desertion by her mother. At twelve she rejoined her father, but because she and her stepmother could not agree, she left and lead a vagabond existence as an adolescent. Two abusive marriages followed. At the outset of therapy she ruminated homicidally about her second husband and could not resolve her past. As part of a comprehensive treatment plan, she was offered a ritual to enact in order psychologically to let go of her second husband and aspects of her abusive past. Drawings that represented earlier traumatic experiences were burned and then buried along with photos and other mementos of her husband. Then she returned home to shower and throw away clothing worn at the burning ceremony. Finally, she ate dinner with a friend. The cleansing ritual she had performed replaced her painful recollections with a feeling of emptiness. As she filled her emptiness with new experiences, her depression lifted and interpersonal contacts increased.

Other metaphorical homework projects aim at enhancing understanding rather than offer a ceremony to facilitate a passage from one life-style to another. Consider a parent whose unacknowledged teasing contributes to a son's disobedient behavior. Such a parent may leave an adult book within "public" access (e.g., on a coffee table). When the curious youngster discovers and reads it, he is punished. Or the parent may leave a cookie jar prominently displayed on the breakfast table. To the child it serves as a cue to ask for a cookie, but doing so leads to angry refusal by the parent. In both examples, the parent is providing more temptation than the child can manage internally and the obvious solution of more discreet placement of forbidden items is being overlooked. The parent can be requested to participate in an experiment, the outcome of which it is hoped will be instructive to the parent for the problem that has been identified with the child.

If the parent is agreeable, the therapist proceeds by writing on a piece of paper that is sealed in an envelope. The parent is instructed that the envelope contains a message that can make life more pleasant at home, but the parent is not to open it until after the next session. However, the parent is asked to carry the envelope at all times. When asked at the next session about his temptations, the parent has the opportunity to empathize more deeply with the child's similar predicament.

A client may be engaging in some particular safe but unsatisfying behavior. The behavior may have been useful at one time, but has outlived its usefulness. Requests to give up the habit in favor of more realistic behavior has not proved helpful. The client can be requested to go to the back of his closet and pull out some old clothes that are no longer worn. The client is to lay out the clothes on the bed and reflect upon how nice they appeared at one point to the client, but how out of date and unfashionable they appear today. The client may even ask, "What did I see in them in the first place?" At the next session, the client can be asked about the experience to solicit the awareness that something that was once fashionable and appropriate can become woefully outdated. Finally, the therapist can help the client to recognize that this is what his symptomatic behavior looks like to others now and may come to look like to the client.

A common client malady consists of having a small repertoire of highly restrictive and well entrenched patterns of behavior from which to derive pleasure. The behavioral expressions may vary between clients, but they share the common outcome of little enjoyment in the client's life. The overly relied upon behaviors have lost their reinforcing qualities through overuse. Life becomes dull, bland, empty. Alternative sources of enjoyment elude awareness. The client is demoralized and depressed. Such a client is usually able to recognize that, while an occasional steak can be rewarding, a steady diet of even steak becomes monotonous. The client can be asked to begin expanding horizons by starting with the palate. Instructions are offered to buy and prepare foods never tried before and to patronize restaurants never before visited. The client can be asked to vary the nationality of new foods sampled each day to maximize contrast. Next session, the client is asked to relate any discoveries about himself in relation to food. Many discover the experience to be highly stimulating. Analogical connections can then be made to other areas of living in order to increase the probability of creating variety and discovering other rewarding activities in which to participate while tried-and-true ones are recharged by disuse.

Verbal Pictures

A picture is worth a thousand words. Seeing is believing. Vision appears to be the primary sensory means by which individuals validate experience. Perhaps that is why therapists frequently appeal to the client's imagination in applying treatment techniques. For example, the covert sensitization techniques of Cautela (1966) successfully combine visual imagery and behavioral techniques to reinforce desirable behavior and extinguish undesirable behavior. Several years before, Wolpe (1958) counterposed anxiety engendering images with relaxation to systematically desensitize anxious individuals.

A therapist can tap the pictures floating through consciousness as he talks with clients to stimulate their thinking, frequently in unexpected ways. To the extent that the therapist is attuned to a particular client, it is likely that seemingly parenthetical images relate analogically. Occasionally, these images can be offered in a way that is thought-provoking or enlightening. For example, a group therapy client had been going through the difficult break up of a relationship. Both he and his former girlfriend were not suited to each other, but continued to visit one another for sex and dependent exploitation. The therapist disclosed the following verbal picture:

> "While you were talking about your relationship with your ex-girlfriend I imagined a Coke bottle half filled with Coke and resting without a cap on it in a refrigerator. It looked like Coke and it tasted like Coke, but the fizz was gone. Can you use this in some way in relation to what you were just talking about?"

The client successfully related the fantasy to his desire to maintain a relationship after the effervescence had left. Soon after he ended the relationship.

Interventions of the form, "I have this picture in my head; how does it relate to your predicament?" stimulate clients to decode the analogical message into cues directly related to their reality issues. In doing so, they provide themselves opportunities to reconceptualize their present framing of their dilemma. In another example, a particularly impulsive individual who justified his self-indulgent activities with "I feel like it" was offered the analogy of a tropism. Specifically, he was informed that he reminded the therapist of the moth's irresistible urge to fly into the light even to its own destruction. The client was asked if he had witnessed the phenomenon and, of course, he had. He was asked if he was willing to settle for that behavior in his life. Because he was not, a discussion followed in which he addressed his free will and his ability to anticipate consequences of his actions in order not to remain mothlike in his life-style. Associations to "moth" may have afforded further projective utility for the client as well.

Variations of the procedure discussed above offer the client a verbal picture of the ways others see the client. A simple structure for this is to say to the individual, "You come across like you're wearing a '_____' ("kick me," "I'll settle for less," "I buckle under intimidation") sign. Is this the way you want to be seen by others?" Another way is to ascribe to the client a social role with all the adornments that vivify the role. For example, an overly accommodating client was informed that the therapist had a picture of her as a hostess and went on at great length about the image. The hostess image had far greater impact than a simple discussion of her tendency to accommodate others at her expense. Later, the client would only have to say, "Do I have my apron on here?" to share with her therapist her awareness of this proclivity. Similarly, an overachieving individual was informed that she was seen as having on a Superwoman cape. Did she want to leave it at home now and again? It is thought that this and other verbal pictures bring words to life by tapping both verbal and visual channels and, by doing so, increase the impact upon the client.

Past Experience as a Metaphor for the Present

Remember a period when you kept at a thing time and time again despite repeated failure until you finally succeeded at it. It does not matter what the occasion was, only that you recall one instance. It may be learning to ride a bicycle, mastering the oboe, or accomplishing three laps of swimming.

Remember in particular the feelings associated with accomplishment that go with the experience. When you are at the point at which you are actually reexperiencing some of the original sensation, ask yourself where else in your current life you can deposit that feeling to encourage you to persevere, despite setbacks, in the hope of eventually replicating the earlier success.

The point is that revivifying prior successes when facing

similar uncertain circumstances can increase current motivation and serve as a foil to discouragement and disillusionment. You are not "talked into" this state of mind; rather, you become your own expert by comparing prior experience to a current one. Similar procedures with clients get them in touch with resources of their own that they may have overlooked. When current impasses in the client's life are related to those of the same form successfully overcome, the client no longer can assume that resolution is impossible; rather, the issue now becomes one of *how*, not if, the client can overcome.

Consider the following examples. A client complains of being fearful of public speaking. The client is asked if she has ever had the experience of being frightened of a thing and then discovering there is no longer any need to be afraid. The client hesitates and then says she has always been afraid of everything. The therapist asks her if she was once afraid of the night, but no longer is. Mildly astonished at a triumph she had not conceptualized as a successful overcoming of a fear, the client responds that she was once terrified of the night and now no longer even feels the least bit anxious when darkness approaches. How does she account for the difference? The client concludes that night has always remained the same, but the client herself has changed so that she no longer feels fear in a situation that once elicited a strong fear reaction. By reevaluating the threat she attached to darkness, she modified her reactions. She is then asked to apply this experience to her current dilemma.

Another client is doubtful of the efficacy of using therapy to reconceptualize past experience to help himself in the present. Why spend time going over something that has already occurred when he is concerned about his present and future? The client is asked by his therapist if he has ever had the experience of reading a poem or book at one time in his life and then rereading it years later to discover that he is able to comprehend it more deeply and meaningfully than he once thought possible. If he has had this experience, he may be able to apply it to the desirability of reinterpreting earlier experiences now that he is older and more able in order to comprehend them in a larger and more realistic context.

A third client reports discouragement. He believes therapy

to be too difficult for him to be successful. He is asked if he has ever had the experience of thinking something is very difficult until he learns how to do it and, once having done so, discovers how easy it can be. The client reports having had greatly doubted his ability to master word processing in his business, but now is an accomplished computer operator in word processing and in other areas as well. He spontaneously relates that he is catastrophizing about his therapy as he tends to do with many new opportunities in his life. He reports that it is helpful for him to hold on to past successes when he becomes self-derogating in order to keep himself motivated for his therapy.

Past experience common to all individuals can also be tapped and applied to present issues, even if the client cannot recall the experience firsthand. For instance, very few people can recall their infancy, but all have had in common many of the experiences now observed in infants. A nonexpressive and constricted client may state that she has "always been this way" or was "born hideously shy." She can be asked if she has ever noticed how freely infants express themselves until they are taught not to. They laugh, cry, and express anger with great intensity and spontaneity. Had she ever seen an infant that did not? Why does she suppose she would have been different? More importantly, how did she learn to curb her natural expressiveness?

Epigrammatic Telegrams

Written epigrammatic messages are related to a phenomenon sometimes referred to as the "talisman effect." Practitioners had observed that noncompliance with prescribed chemotherapy was epidemic among some segments of the mentally ill. However, when the clients were given something tangible they could take with them from their therapy, compliance increased greatly. The object may take the form of a written appointment card or a written explanation of their medication or therapy. Regardless of its nature, the giving of some material appeared to be the crucial factor. Similarly, psychotherapy clients may derive more benefit from their therapy if they are provided an occasional written message pertinent to their therapy.

It is thought that the benefit of written communication can

be enhanced by applying the principle of incompleteness mentioned earlier. That is, a brief message, ambiguously or metaphorically related to a current therapeutic dilemma, is thought to be more engaging and less readily dismissed than an obvious one. Moreover, especially provocative are those to which the client is unable to respond until the next therapy hour. The client is put in the position not only of mustering an argument against the therapist's communication, but also of actively maintaining the objection until the next session. When most successful, the "telegram" usually results in a client wanting to prove the therapist wrong, but as he considers it over the interval between sessions, actually comes to accept it as useful. For these reasons, these communications are thought to have optimal impact if given to the client at the conclusion of a session in a sealed envelope. The client is instructed not to open the envelope until reaching home and if he has any questions about the contents, please to bring them up at the next session.

Here are some examples:

A teenager bitterly resented his mother's awakening him for school, but would frequently be late for school without her intervention. At the end of a session, he was given the following message sealed in an envelope: "If you don't like being told what to do, then do it before you have to be told." The client reported he at first resented the therapist "siding" with his mother. The more he thought about it, however, the more he realized that he had control over how much she intruded in his life. By the fourth day he had bought an alarm clock.

Another client complained of intense dissatisfaction and malaise over the elusiveness of rewarding experiences in her life. At the same time, she would turn the direction of her life over to luck, fate, or to others whom she saw as more powerful and competent than herself. At the end of an hour she was given a sealed envelope. She was informed that something was written inside that related to her problem, but she would likely not know how. She was further informed that its usefulness to her in therapy would come only from her studying it until she recognized the relationship, rather than wait for the therapist or others to interpret it for her. Inside was written the notable quote of

Louis Pasteur: "Chance favors the prepared mind." For the next several weeks she attempted to persuade the therapist to interpret it for her rather than struggle with it herself. As he politely but firmly refused to do so, she finally deciphered the personal meaning on her own. Having done so, she recognized that even here in relation to the quote she attempted to tap the resources of others, but success for her came from doing it herself rather than wait for luck to intervene or others to volunteer their resources.

A young adult professed great inadequacy in relation to others. Her parents had attempted to motivate her toward greater success by telling her how her current achievements fell short of the mark. With constant repetition, she had come to believe she was nearly incompetent. She accepted her inferiority as a fact rather than as a misattribution that required her complicity to retain its potency. A turning point in her therapy occurred when she was given the written message (originating with Eleanor Roosevelt) on a piece of scrap paper at the end of an hour: "No one can make you inferior without your consent." With one statement, she enabled herself to recapture her individuality, her separateness from the influence of her parents, and move toward more independent living.

Another client tended to believe uncritically almost anything someone told her. She came to therapy because she frequently felt used unfairly by others. Her naivete and suggestibility were thought to play a prominent role in her victimization. Toward the end of a therapy hour that she had spent despairing over others misrepresenting themselves to her, she was offered a riddle popularized by Abraham Lincoln. "If you call a dog's tail a leg, how many legs does a dog have?" She was given the answer in a sealed envelope. However, she was requested to give the riddle a great deal of thought and only after she had derived a satisfactory answer herself was she to look up the answer provided by Lincoln. When she compared her answer of five legs to Lincoln's ("A dog continues to have four legs. Calling a dog's tail a leg does not make it so"), she was able to see more clearly how she tended to act as though a tail were a leg in her own life as well.

Etymological Approaches

Words and idiomatic expressions are actually metaphors in many cases. A new idea is described in terms of other experiences with which the listener is familiar. For example, "to learn" comes from an Indo-European word meaning "furrow" or "track." To learn something is to stay on track. "To go out of furrow" is *delirare* in Latin, from which "delirium" is derived.

With overuse, words and idioms have become clichés to the extent that the impact of their original meanings is lost. Individuals are so familiar with the abstraction that the literal activity that forms the basis of the concept is overlooked. At times individuals literally do not know what they are saying. A client may complain of being "down in the dumps," "broken-hearted," "having a splitting headache," among a wide variety of other words and phrases that are richly descriptive and psychologically telling, without being aware of the relationship of these expressions to the psychological processes they represent. The intention of this therapeutic modality, then, is metaphor in reverse. That is, the goal of the therapist is to take the expression of the client and make it fresh and impactive once again by relating the abstraction to its roots and the roots to the client's dilemma. In this way, the client has an opportunity to reconceptualize the experiences represented by his word choice.

Few individuals are aware, or need be, that the expression "I am" actually translates to "I breathe" in the Sanskrit from which it is derived. To an individual suffering from depersonalization symptoms associated with hyperventilation, however, the association between breathing and loss of appreciation of oneself can have major overtones. The individual may derive comfort from an association, long established, that demystifies the relationship of overbreathing to changes in personal awareness. Almost certainly the originators did not have this particular association between breathing and being in mind, but that there *is* an association is an important link to one seeking a "normal" explanation for the feeling of "going crazy." This same process of identifying associational links between words and experiences for clients can have a facilitating effect in a wide variety of situations. Several clients have spontaneously remarked on the high

interest value of the word origins and how such interest facilitated a new appreciation for the meaning inherent in their own
statements. A few examples of word origins that can become
highly relevant to clients are offered here.

A commonly encountered client phenomenon is a capacity
for substituting one feeling state for another. The substitution
may protect the client from the discomfort associated with the
dissociated feeling, but hinders successful resolution of the conflict associated with the estranged emotion. Knowledge of the
common etymological origin of the three difficult emotional
states of anger, anxiety, and anguish may persuade the client of
the capacity for substituting one related feeling for another.
Thus the anxious individual may be able to make a connection to
repressed grief or rage. The belligerent client who acts angry
when he feels hurt can legitimize dealing with the hurt underlying the anger.

Our modern word "anger" is derived from the Old Norse
angr which means "grief." It is related to the Latin *angor* meaning "anguish" and the Sanskrit *amhas* which means "anxiety."

The word "companion" has been traced to the Latin phrase
cum panis ("break bread with") and can be used effectively with
lonely individuals who profess to be at a loss in making friends.
The origin of companionship literally prescribes sharing and
taking a meal together as a basis of friendship.

Some overweight individuals enter treatment after experiencing failure with a series of diets. They appear to interpret
the diet as a temporary modification of their eating habits that,
once completed, signals a resumption of old patterns of unre-
strained food intake. Providing these clients with an explanation
of the origin of "diet" can, with the receptive individual, dissolve
the misconception. It comes from the Greek *diaitan* which means
"to lead one's life" or "to govern." In this manner, a diet is rein-
terpreted as a way of living rather than a hiatus from familiar
eating habits and, equally importantly, it accents the necessity of
taking control of one's own impulses rather than indulging in
them.

Avoidance of necessary confrontation is occasionally rationalized by an individual as a justifiable act of kindness rather than
understood as an expression of insecurity. Our cultural edict of

"If you don't have something nice to say, then say nothing at all," if applied generally, is such an example. Consider the example of a friend who is experimenting with a new style of dress before an important event. She asks the opinion of a confidant in order to achieve honest feedback on which to base modifications. The garment she is wearing is not nearly as flattering as another in her wardrobe. Her friend, responding to her own desire to maintain their friendship and boost the confidence of her nervous intimate, tells her she looks wonderful. Later, when the other recognizes the well-intentioned deceit, her confidence is shaken in her friendship with the "nice" person.

For such individuals who are nice to the extent that they earn low marks from others who wish honesty more than flattery, the original meaning of niceness may help take their justification out of the realm of virtuous conduct. The mildly positive connotations for niceness are quite new. As recently as Shakespeare's time nice meant "foolish" as derived from the Old French where it meant "stupid." Both have a common ancestry with the Latin word *nescius* which means "ignorance."

"Respect" actually means "to look again." This literal meaning proved helpful to a client who tended to give away her self-respect by being overly accommodating to others, as well as self-effacing. She had achieved an excellent intellectual understanding of her depression as being a predictable consequence of acting on these tendencies. In order to regain her self-respect she was agreeable to look again at (re-spect) her inclinations before taking action, in order to determine if the outcome would be self-enhancing or self-deflating. In this way she could pause before acting to judge the behavior in terms of self-interest. The literal meaning of respect was sufficiently impactive to her that it served as an outstanding prompt to maintain her integrity through self-reflection, to the extent that little other effort was required to maintain her positive change.

Idiomatic expressions and slang are rich sources of client subliminal expertise that can be brought to the client's attention with often dramatic results. For example, a client who complains of "being in a rut" can be asked how actual ruts are formed on a surface. When the client responds that ruts are the outcome of repetitive movement, the therapist may ask the client to relate this principle to the routine in his own life.

Just as an expression of speech can be defined in terms of the operations necessary to perform the function (as in the rut-forming example), so also may abstract words be operationally defined. Highly abstract concepts like truth, honor, and justice, often become only loosely tied to the referents they seek to describe. A great deal of uncertainty and ambiguity can result for the individual and for others as well. For example, a client may complain of being unable to trust a partner. However, the client is unable to specify a meaning of trust that will enable him to determine if the partner has acted in an untrustworthy manner. If the client can be guided to define trust as the "matching of statements and behavior," then he has a clear criterion by which to evaluate the behavior of the partner, and the partner has a clear guide for actions and verbalizations. A similar definitional approach has been helpful for clients who define a concept in a one-sided manner. For example, a conscience-ridden and hyper-dutiful individual defined fairness as "not exploiting others." A more balanced and complete definition of "not exploiting others and not letting others exploit you" gave sanction to greater limit setting without guilt.

A number of words in the English language are compound; that is, they are formed by combining two or more distinct morphological elements. "Overturn" is an example. Made up of two simple words, it has come to be synonymous with "invalidate," an abstraction only remotely related to turning something over. Through repetitive use, the abstraction from the combination of two words takes on a character of its own, frequently obscuring the original usage. "Death knell" no longer necessarily refers to the literal tolling of a church bell at the death of a Christian; rather, its meaning has generalized to any act that puts an end to anything.

When a client uses a word with insufficient consideration for what is being said, a facilitating effect can frequently be achieved by referring the client to the actual meaning of the word being used. Consider these examples:

A client complained of being too discouraged to engage in a new activity despite lamenting a life of being on the outside looking in at others having fun. The therapist judged the client to be capable of engaging in the activity, but suspected the client was fearful of acceptance. The therapist wrote "dis + courage" on a piece of paper and asked the client to identify what "discourage" actually meant. The client said he wasn't sure. The therapist asked if he knew what the "dis" in "distrust" added to the concept of "trust." The client correctly replied it meant "not to trust." He was asked again if he could identify the meaning of discourage, and correctly answered that it can mean not having enough courage, and that discouragement can be dissolved by acts of courage. With reassurance, he took part in the activity and enjoyed himself immensely.

Another client frequently did what others wanted her to do even though she did not want to. While this behavior both demoralized and depressed her, she rationalized it by saying that not to do so would be inconsiderate of others. She was asked, straight-faced, if she knew what "consider" meant. She responded that it meant "to think about something." She was enjoined to use this knowledge to redefine "considerate" and "inconsiderate." To her satisfaction, she decided that "considerate" means to think about the interests of others before deciding what she wants to do, but it in no way implies that she is to do what others want her to do on all occasions.

A harried businessman sought therapy because he could no longer organize his work well. The longer his hours, the less he appeared to accomplish. He showed a number of symptoms of burnout and it was thought that a short vacation would reduce stress and be reinvigorating. He was asked to take some time off for recreation. As expected, he replied he could not take the time off, even though his energies were depleted. The therapist wrote "re + creation" on a blackboard and asked the businessman why he thinks we call "recreation" and "re-creation" by the same word. By the end of the therapy hour he felt comfortable taking time away from work as it would "recharge" his resources to complete more work in the long run. After a week's vacation he was quite refreshed.

Teaching Stories

A story is an elaborate metaphor. Characters and plots dramatize fundamental aspects of the human dilemma. Myths and legends have enduringly transmitted various cultural mores and human insights down the ages of humankind. A story may successfully communicate an idea where rational discussion of the same theme can fail. Jessamyn West has remarked, "Fiction reveals truths that reality obscures." With a story one can sharply focus the significant portions of human dilemmas to be amplified while minimizing other aspects not central to the purpose. Simplification and amplification are exploited by the storyteller to bring home a point. A story line holds interest. The visual imagery augments the impact of communication whether written or verbally transmitted. Additionally, the story can work subliminally at an allegorical level. One acheives an understanding that is profound and life-modifying, although it frequently escapes conscious symbolization in words. When one reads *The Ugly Duckling* to a child who feels left out and alienated, the child feels heartened and renewed. The child cannot put the help readily into words, but the impact is powerful.

Storytelling as a therapeutic tool is becoming increasingly practiced by professional psychotherapists (see Brandell, 1984, for a review) either in the form of eliciting stories from clients or of offering stories to them. The present discussion is limited to therapist-transmitted teaching stories to fit the context of this chapter, but this limited range is not intended to impugn the efficacy of client-related stories. A collection of instructive stories for children has been written by Gardner (1977) and the teaching tales of Milton Erickson have been compiled by Rosen (1982). The interested reader will be richly rewarded by reviewing these sources of teaching stories.

Perhaps the greatest asset of the teaching story for a client is that it communicates a principle at least one step removed from emotionally laden conflict. By approaching a client indirectly, it is hoped defenses are bypassed and the message registered from this safe distance. The acknowledged principles illustrated in the story then can be applied to the reality issues of the client. Consider this dramatization (originating with Glen King) to help a client increase his understanding of client complicity in being used by others:

Client: It seems like I do all the giving in my relationship and wind up getting used over and over again. I don't get it.
Therapist: Let's stop for a minute. I'd like to tell you a story

and see if there is something in there that relates to this issue. Suppose a person goes up to a bar and orders a drink. Someone sits down beside this person and says, "Be a sport and buy me a drink."

So the person buys a drink for the stranger. A few minutes later, the individual feels a tap on his shoulder followed by a request for another drink. The request is honored. This goes on for a few more drinks. Then, without a word, the stranger leaves the bar. What did the person who bought the drinks get from the other individual?

Client: Nothing.

Therapist: What did he ask for?

Client: Nothing.

Therapist [matter-of-factly]: He got what he asked for. What value do we place on things given away for free?

Client [becoming more alert as he registers the principle in relation to himself]: Very little.

Therapist: Then what value do you suppose the guy who got the free drinks places on the buyer?

Client: Not much at all.

Therapist: How do you suppose others who watched this transaction in the bar see the buyer?

Client: I'd guess they see him as kind of a fool.

Therapist: When you get taken advantage of by others, do you feel kind of foolish?

Client: Very. I was seeing me as that guy at the bar. I'm not liking what I see.

Therapist: What does the guy at the bar need to do to see himself differently?

Client: He needs to not give just because someone asks, especially when he doesn't have something to show for it.

Therapist: I'm sensing that you're talking about yourself here.

Other stories can simplify or exaggerate, even to the point of parody, a dilemma facing a client, in the hope of encouraging spontaneous reconceptualization. One such story addresses the issue of "niceness" discussed in the previous section. A young adult had great difficulty asserting herself effectively with others out of concern for hurting their feelings. She was offered this story.

A woman was asked out on a date. She liked the man all right, but she knew he was not her type. But he had asked, and she didn't want to hurt his feelings, so she said she would go out with him. They went out to dinner and a show and she had a rather good time. At the end of the evening, he leaned over to kiss her goodnight. She did not even want to go out on the date, much less kiss him good night! However, he did buy dinner and tickets and she had no "good reason" to turn him down and it would hurt his feelings if she refused. So she kissed him and hoped he would never call again.

What do you suppose happened? Sure enough, he asked her out for a date again. She knew he would be crushed if she said no because she had kissed him, and she had no "good reason" to say no, so she accepted. Again she had quite a good time, although she still knew he was not her type and it could not become serious. Toward the end of the night he made a small advance. She did not want to "make out," but he would be disappointed and what harm was there in it? So she allowed petting.

The weeks went by and she kept accepting. One day he professed his love to her and his desire to make love to her. She could go on no further. She told him she did not want to date him, that they were not right for each other. He was crestfallen, shocked, and disheartened, asking her what had "happened." He left her doorstep on the point of tears. Both felt miserable.

What do you suppose she did then? She felt so bad about what she had done, she called him back and agreed to marry him. He felt better. She felt better—temporarily. The day of the wedding she became panicky. She could not let him down after all she had said and done. She went through with the wedding. About 2 years later and after the birth of their child she realized she could stand no more. She told him she would have to leave and she did. Both felt miserable for a long time to come.

The story proved useful to elucidate for the client how attempts to shelter individuals from small hurts can lead to greater ones. She came to an understanding that she was unintentionally misleading others in her attempts to spare both herself and others embarrassment or disappointment. She also achieved a more mature understanding of interactions and relationships. That is, she accepted that the risk one takes to engage others is to absorb the small disappointments associated with having overtures rejected. As a recipient of an overture, one's obligation in return is to respond truthfully and tactfully.

Therapeutic stories frequently have as their objective the presentation of an alternative frame of reference from which to understand an experience. The following is a story offered to a highly competent midwestern engineer who persistenlty saw herself as a failure and unacceptable to others. She would mock herself by saying she was born without "the right stuff" and was a "professional imposter" who, upon discovery by her peers, would be drummed out of her profession. With others she came across as "all business," displaying little willingness to let the warm and soft aspects of her personality show. She shielded her vulnerability from detection by belittling and structuring relationships in terms of control. She had great difficulty in letting others give to her. However, her chronic dysphoria gave away her tremendous dissatisfaction.

Painful exploration in therapy revealed her upbringing by an apparently hypercritical father who did not know how to get close to his only daughter. When she tried to show warmth and caring toward him he insensitively rejected her overtures time and time again. As a result, she appeared to protect herself from anticipated rejection by reproving others first. When they would retreat, she would confirm the false hypothesis that it is better to avoid emotional involvement with others because they will leave her anyway. Her therapist believed that she would have to reconceptualize her early experience with her father as something missing in him rather than as something missing in her. With anxiety then reduced, she could risk reaching out emotionally to others once again and more realistically appraise her self-worth. To facilitate this reconceptualization she was offered the following story in written form at the end of a session:

The Story of the Girl with the Basket of Apples

There was a girl who, through no fault of her own, had to move from her own country to a foreign land. She had no choice in the matter. Apples were highly regarded in her home country because they were tasty and nutritious. She took some applies with her to use to make friends.

When she arrived in the new country she met stranger after stranger and offered each an apple. But each one refused. They had no apples in their country, had never seen an apple, and didn't know how to eat one, or whether it would be good.

After a while the girl stopped offering her apples and believed that what she had to offer was not worthwhile. She did not realize that the problem was the strangers' unfamiliarity with apples, and not in the little girl who offered them.

It was hoped that the fairytale language of the story would appeal to the little girl part of herself that carried the hypothesized fear of rejection of her giving. Unfortunately, she was unable to continue in her therapy due to a move from the area and the effectiveness of this particular intervention has not been assessed with her directly. However, not long after leaving, her therapist discovered she had begun volunteer work at a shelter for abused women.

Another example of a teaching story to facilitate reconceptualization actively involves the client during the telling of the tale. Here is an example that has proven helpful to many individuals who place others in an awkward position by not allowing themselves to be cared about (after an idea by Glen King):

Therapist: Suppose you were sick, and a neighbor from down the street showed up one day to help. She mowed your lawn, brought you chicken soup and had the evening paper tucked under her arm for you. Would you feel cared about?

Client [emphatically]: I'd feel very cared about.

Therapist: Suppose you recover, and a few weeks later you discover your neighbor broke her leg and is laid up in her house. What would you like to do about it, if anything?

Client: I'd like to reciprocate. I owe her and I'd like to pay her back.

Therapist: All right. Let's suppose you show up at her house dragging a lawn mower with a jar of chicken soup in the other hand, and today's paper in your mouth. You announce you're here to help. She replies that she has called Meals-on-Wheels who will bring food daily. She has arranged for the delivery boy to bring the paper to her room. She has paid a neighborhood kid to mow the lawn. How are you feeling?

Client: I'd feel disappointed.

Therapist: Why?

Client: She helped me. I wanted to help her.

Therapist: Because she won't let you care for her you have a debt you can't pay back. It just keeps mounting. How comfortable are you going to feel around her after awhile?

Client: Not very. It makes me not want to accept anything from her until we get it more equal.

Therapist: If you can see it with the woman in the story, then see it with yourself. Some may react to their discomfort by backing off as a means to reduce the discomfort. How do you think exploitive individuals would react?

Client: I think they'd just keep taking as much as I'd give.

Therapist: Say, isn't that what you've told me happens to you: The nice guys eventually leave and the duds keep hanging on? Do you think this might have something to do with it?

"Responsibility" means literally "the ability to make responses." A client can be helped to act more responsibly by being offered uncommon and thought-provoking interventions that create opportunities for expanded behavioral repertoires. The more options an individual has available from which to choose, the more discriminating he can become. Therapeutic experiments, metaphorical homework, verbal pictures, metaphorical usage of one's past, epigrams, etymological approaches, and storytelling are all geared to aid in reconceptualization. It is believed that such a restructuring of experience is frequently a necessary precursor to real and lasting behavioral change.

At times the most carefully thought out intervention appears to encounter resistance that threatens to stagnate the therapeutic process. The next chapter attempts to deal with this issue.

CHAPTER 6

RESISTANCE AND RECONCEPTUALIZATION
Making the Familiar Unfamiliar

The greatest victor wins without a battle.

—Lao Tzu

With few exceptions, clients actually fight the means to achieve treatment goals while simultaneously exerting often courageous attempts to improve themselves. This resistance may vary greatly in degree, but almost always increases the more a therapist attempts to force a particular client to do what is "good" for him (see Sherman, 1980, pp. 74-75). Riebel (1984) has categorized resistance as occurring on two levels. Resistance on an individual level is the client's reluctance to make use of the help he has requested. On a systemic level, resistance is a family's (or other group's) attempt to remain the same. The manifestations of resistance are legion, but share in common the phenomenon of avoidance of what the therapist believes to be relevant.

The Tendency to Preserve the Status Quo

Why does acceptance of modification come with such great difficulty? Thomas Kuhn (1962) asked this question in regard to the great opposition even empirically derived innovation encounters when challenging conventionally held scientific theory (which he calls "normal science"). His insightful book, *The Structure of Scientific Revolution*, by analogy is instructive to understanding resistance encountered in psychotherapy. Kuhn's study of the history of scientific thought revealed "novelty emerges only with great difficulty, manifested by resistance, against a backdrop of expectation" (p. 64).

The pivotal discovery that supported the conclusion was that normal science is predicated upon the assumption that the established scientific community already knows what the world is like. Experimentation, in large measure, seeks to confirm the assumptions; novel findings are frequently suppressed because they subvert the basic commitments of normal science (p. 5). Initially, only the anticipated is likely to be even detected under circumstances where anomaly is later to be observed (p. 64). Continued exposure to repeated anomaly erodes the conventional interpretation of nature to the extent that anomaly is not only recognized, but also gains in support (pp. 77-84). Eventually, a crisis or impasse between the innovative finding and normal science requires resolution in one of three ways:

1. Normal science ultimately proves able to handle the anomaly; therefore, the innovation is rejected.
2. The problem is set aside for future generations.
3. The paradigm itself can undergo modification to account for the new finding and incorporate others.

Like the proponents of established scientific conventions, many clients begin therapy invested in models of the world that are assumed to be the proper if not the only interpretation of experience. New experiences are more readily incorporated into existing preconceptions or incompatible data ignored or distorted than the model itself modified.

Imagine a scientist who has dedicated his professional life to the "proper" investigation of phenomena, often at great self-sacrifice. How difficult it must be to be confronted with a new formulation that challenges, if not negates, a lifetime of effort.

Who would quarrel with the scientist's skepticism, strenuous efforts to test the reconceptualization for flaws, or time required to digest emotionally the impact of the discovery before aligning with the new direction because of its greater utility? Similarly, individuals spend a lifetime molding and refining a personal understanding of the world, the challenging of which confronts the client with awareness of much loss or hurt that could have been minimized, if not prevented, had the modification only come sooner. Many react to an alternative reformulation as an intrusion or personal affront requiring an adequate defense.

An exceptional example of resistance to change occurred with a fifty-eight year-old man we shall call Mr. Caldwell. He had been referred to the clinic by vocational rehabilitation services because of "inability to cope with stress and depression." His inability manifested itself by antagonism and abrasiveness to even minor challenges to his model of the world. He spent his first therapy hour lambasting the "establishment" and all who had not seen eye to eye with him over a lifetime. His statements were liberally peppered with vulgarities and obscenities. When asked what he would like to have from his therapist he angrily responded that he should not have to be "detailed to death" about what he needs because the therapist was the expert and he had only a fifth-grade education. Further, the therapist should know him well enough to "second guess" him accurately. However, his manner of speech was idiosyncratic to the point of being obscure and nearly incomprehensible.

His vulgar speech appeared to be a means of keeping others at a distance, as did his antagonism. He habitually made himself almost unintelligible to others. Despite his many and varied attempts to alienate his therapist, and his repudiation and disdain for all institutions, he not only met his initial appointment, but also did not leave the office until the therapist terminated the session. Further, he returned weekly for scheduled appointments.

Over the course of several sessions he revealed that he held strong views which he was unwilling to change. One of these positions was "It's going to be my way or no way" which he regularly practiced during the course of his three marriages, the rearing of his children, and his tenure as an auto mechanic. His inability to compromise or negotiate with others necessitated another strongly held principle—that of self-reliance.

Unfortunately, Mr. Caldwell contracted several physical ailments that undermined these two fundamental tenets of his philosophy of life. Cataracts were increasingly depriving him of his eyesight. However, he continually refused corrective surgery offered free because he wanted "no strings"—although none were attached. His emphysema had worsened to the extent that he could no longer work in the vicinity of car fumes. Mr. Caldwell was relieved of his job against his will. He continued to smoke heavily despite the great strain on his system and acute resulting discomfort. When referred to vocational rehabilitation services, he alienated himself until he was dropped from the program and referred for psychotherapy. He appeared to view his participation as a loss of dignity. He had applied for disability benefits and then arranged to be turned down by purposely telling the administrative law judge he had strung 400 catfish lines (qualifying him as a commercial catfisherman) even though he was unable to maintain his lines because of left arm numbness, chest pain, and insufficient stamina. He justified his actions by stating that "400 lines wasn't enough to make a living off of anyway." When pressed, he equated receiving disability benefits with "being a bum." Although under medical care for his condition, he did not comply with treatment and necessitated a transfer from one physician to another after striking the doctor who insisted he change his life-style to arrest his deteriorating condition. The onset of his depression appeared to be associated with his increased dependency due to physical limitations.

Mr. Caldwell possessed a particularly rigid model of the world. A common denominator across a wide range of phenomena appeared to be his pathologically high valuation of independence from the influence of others. His extreme views prohibited him from being able to ask for or accept help from others without feeling devalued or humiliated—even with his life at stake. Two therapeutic goals were to enable him to quit smoking in order to maximize his health status and to obtain disability benefits in order to maximize his independence. The challenge was one of influencing an individual with an intractable worldview, a central axis of which was resisting influence of others.

He had moved in with his son after his latest divorce and resented his dependency upon his son's finances. When the therapist linked his cigarette dependency to his reliance upon his son's finances, he defended his smoking vociferously. He angrily asserted that smoking was a habit and that the therapist had habits of his own. When the therapist calmly replied that he paid for his habits, Mr. Caldwell countered that his son earned enough money to support both himself and the client's smoking. The therapist responded that the amount of his son's income is a separate issue from his dependency upon his son's money to support his habit.

Mr. Caldwell shifted to accusing the therapist of being responsible for his smoking in the office because of the availability of an ashtray on the table beside him. The therapist allowed that dependent people might weaken and buckle at the sight of a cue for smoking but his nonsmoking clients did not feel compelled to light up at the sight of his powerful ashtray. Mr. Caldwell next assailed the therapist's motives for urging him to quit smoking, declaring that the therapist was getting back at him because he was offended by his behavior. Furthermore, the therapist was looking for an excuse to drop him from treatment. The therapist responded that he was welcome in therapy whether he quit or not and that he would have to accept responsibility for dropping out of treatment if he wished to do so. In an equally obscure vein, Mr. Caldwell went on to justify his smoking as a means of keeping his physician in business and a means for his son to pay him back for his fathering. The therapist listened patiently before announcing that all this was irrelevant to whether he would be willing to give up smoking. Finally, the client stated he was unwilling to stop smoking and for the therapist to quit "harassing" him. The therapist replied that was what he needed to hear to stop, adding that he was worn out and unable to influence him.

Within 2 weeks, Mr. Caldwell stopped smoking. On occasion he would bring in a cigarette to let the therapist know he had not been influenced. Apparently, Mr. Caldwell was able to reconceptualize smoking as an intolerable dependency while also reconciling his refusal to be influenced by others through outlasting efforts to modify his behavior by one whom he defined as more authoritative than himself. Several months later, Mr. Caldwell resumed smoking at a time when he was having difficulty soliciting conformity to his wishes from his girlfriend.

His defense of smoking as a means of allowing others to repay a debt afforded an opportunity for him to grant himself disability benefits for which he was eminently qualified. He had been hospitalized a few years previously to have a lung removed. He was asked if his wife came to visit him in the hospital. Characteristically, he related how he angrily rejected her visits as doing no good. He was chided for depriving her of the opportunity to give him some support in exchange for the financial support he had given her over their years together. Worse yet, he was not allowing himself to repay a debt to himself. He had contributed to Social Security throughout his working life and now would not use it. Following extensive discussion along this line, he was requested to give permission to the therapist to petition the Social Security office for a rehearing. The request was granted. He could not ask for himself, but would allow another to ask for him as long as it was done in the context of repaying himself. In time, he allowed his therapist to arrange for his cataract surgery which was successfully performed a year after it had been initially offered. Mr. Caldwell remained a prisoner of his model of the world, but at least he was able to achieve a degree of latitude within it.

There is a cartoon in which the frog prince confronts his lady fair from his lily pad. The maiden's downcast face registers her displeasure as the frog says, "But I don't want to be turned into a prince. I want you to accept me as I am." The speaker in the cartoon wants to be treated like a prince while behaving like a frog, both wanting acceptance without doing what it takes to win acceptance. In similar fashion, many clients enter therapy to "get better" but to do so without making changes. An extreme example of this is a bridge phobic whose initial goal in therapy was to develop a scheme to have bridges removed from her area rather than deal with the reality issues for her that surrounded her phobia.

In many cases the resistance can be best understood as inflexibility in the client's model of the world, as in the cases of Mr. Caldwell and the bridge phobic. On another level, resistance can also be understood as a reaction to uncertainty that may influence the individual to hold on to whatever partial solutions are yielded by the current model of the world. Any new undertaking can be accompanied by both hopes for improvement and fears of greater deterioration, by motivation for change and resistance to change. The safe, but unsatisfying, solutions to life's problems predicted by faulty or limited conceptual models are likely compromises that are defended in order to protect against greater losses of satisfaction.

For other clients, symptoms appear to be expressions of security. Losing symptoms may be interpreted as giving up part of oneself. A client may be more motivated to change if the change is structured as becoming more of who the client already is as opposed to losing a symptom. The secondary gain value of symptoms (sympathy, worker's compensation, control over others) is frequently associated with resistance to change. And what if the client tried to change and change was not forthcoming? Few people would condemn an individual for attempting to protect himself against further demoralization.

For these reasons and others, a client's inflexible, faulty, and limiting conceptualizations can be vigorously defended. The first line of defense is to attempt to account for new input within the currently held conceptual framework in much the same manner "normal science" attempts to handle anomaly. The experience of the client form the therapist's side of the relationship is that of a person both genuinely wanting to feel better while also not wanting to change.

The reader is asked to entertain the example of a young housewife referred for depression. At one point she conceived of wifely love as requiring "putting your husband's needs before your own." The conceptualization not only justified her nonassertive selflessness, but also raised it to the level of virtue. Unfortunately, a predictable consequence of giving away her sources of self-worth was depression. As her reaction to objectionable treatment by her husband was explored, she discovered her initial reaction to his behavior was one of anger ("That's not fair"). The uncomfortable sensations associated with anger were effectively relieved by minimization and rationalization ("It's not that bad. He's been under a strain"). Once she minimized the actions of her husband to account for her emotional reaction, she was left to account for her anger in terms of her wifeliness ("I'm just being selfish and demanding.") The emotional concomitants of this conceptualization of her difficulty were depression and even greater selflessness. A vicious cycle had begun. Her defenses were like going one step forward (relief from discomfort) while going two steps backward (they all but guaranteed future objectionable behavior from her husband, greater depression for her, and no change in her resources to deal with similar situations in the future). Like an addictive drug, her reliance upon status quo conceptualization allowed her to experience immediate relief from uncomfortable assaults to her security. The negative side effects were insidious, subtle, even virulent. They were not readily associated with the precipitant.

These feelings associated with resistance can include vulnerability, shame, weakness, ambivalence, resentment, inadequacy, humiliation, embarrassment, and anxiety among others. The false hypothesis that the defensive strategy confirms actually maintains the status quo. It becomes likely that the individual will continue to rely upon the coping strategy within a more rigidly held, albeit faulty, conceptual system.

REMOVING THERAPIST OBSTACLES TO CLIENT TRANSFORMATION

To speak of client resistance is pejorative, as the behavior described is the experience of the client from the therapist point of view. Resistance could also be described as "anything the therapist does that results in a client defending a faulty model of the world." By doing so the onus for resistance shifts to the therapist. Gottman and Leiblum (1974, p. 102) report that beginning therapists tend to blame nonconforming clients for being "resistant" rather than reexamine their own expectations of "good" client behavior. To the extent that this occurs in ongoing therapy, the client is held accountable for therapist inflexibility in therapeutic approach. This iatrogenic resistance occurs in at least five areas: expectations for client role, expectations for client performance, countertransference, timing of interventions, and the content of therapist-provided contact.

It is an unreasonable expectation to wish for clients to conform to one's expectations or for those with problems in living to act as though they have none. Even in the most highly motivated client, a degree of resistance is likely to occur as a by-product of the structure of the therapeutic relationship. For example, an individual who requests therapy to become self-sufficient or self-regulating necessarily is placed in a partially dependent role of requesting help from a therapist.

When a therapist demands client conformity to an expected role, the issue in therapy shifts from one of the client assuming responsibility for himself to one of compliance with authority. The focus is no longer self-regulation; rather, it is one of obedience or disobedience. Under these circumstances, one way a client has to become more independent is by rejecting therapy!

A therapist may have expectations for client performance that are either too high or too low. If expectations are too high, the client experiences demoralization and may give up trying for improvement. On the other hand, if the therapist treats the client as fragile, the client may expect too little of himself and too much from others.

At other times, therapist expectancies for client behavior may be in accord with the client's capabilities, but the timing of the request is out of synchronization with the client's pace through therapy. The transtheoretical model of psychotherapy of Prochaska and DiClemente (1982) is instructive in this regard. It will be recalled their work identified either consciousness-raising, catharsis, decision making, and action to be the emphasis of 18 effective therapies. Each area of emphasis appears to be an important contribution to a comprehensive therapy. That is, regardless of a therapist's conceptual orientation, operationally many effective therapists help a client to increase awareness which in turn facilitates a cathartic experience. At this point or afterwards, the client makes a decision to change and is receptive to implementing these changes. A therapist who urges a client to make choices or implement new behavior before a client has modified his awareness sufficiently to justify the changes is inviting resistance. A therapist who continues to encourage additional insight when the client is prepared to act upon obtained insights is also unintentionally encouraging resistance. In short, what is sometimes referred to as client resistance is likely more correctly labeled as a therapist pacing error.

The word choice of therapists dramatically influences the interpretation of statements by clients. Consider the description of a yellow fluid in a cup as lemonade-colored or urine-colored. Both are accurate denotatively, yet because of the different connotations they result in far different reactions. Because of connotative meaning, the "framing" of therapist feedback interacts with a client's model of the world to determine if it will be received as partisan support, neutral observation, insult, accusation, or criticism. By way of illustration, a simple request for a client to sign an authorization form to receive services can be presented as either an exercise in submission or a free choice. Notice your reaction to the following statements if they were put to you:

> "Would you be willing to sign this form in order to let me work with you?"
> "In order to receive services from me, this form needs to be signed."
> "It's time to sign this form."
> "I'll let you sign this now."
> "Sign this form for me, would you?"
> "You have to sign this form."

Do you notice a different emotional impact of each phrasing? It is beyond the scope of this chapter to pursue this highly interesting area. However, the reader is encouraged to read Hayakawa (1972) for a thoughtful discussion of the interaction of language and thought in general, Rudestam (1978) for the interaction of a client's semantic structure with his or her perception of self and the world, and Wachtel (1980) for the effects of therapist wording of statements upon the client.

An illustration from Wachtel is offered here to demonstrate how therapist phrasing of comments can be productive or counterproductive. A young woman was experiencing conflict with her boyfriend because she would not engage in intercourse. Her claim that the reason for this was her religious belief appeared to her therapist, for a variety of reasons, to be a rationalization. A head-on confrontation of the individual's religious beliefs (e.g., "You think you're doing this for religious reasons, but really it's because you're afraid") may provoke a stalwart defense of one's faith and further crystallize an errant conceptualization. The following is Wachtel's suggested response: "It sounds like certainly one of the reasons you're reluctant to have intercourse is that you feel sex before marriage is bad; but I have the impression you're also beginning to sense that you have a lot of anxiety about having sex with a man."

The statement accepts the stated belief as a motivation in her reluctance (instead of taking it away from her) and adds to it the possibility of anxiety about sex with a man as a motivator as well. Not only is the issue of religion avoided, but also *the client* is given credit for the idea of sexual anxiety as a factor in her reluctance. Once sexual anxiety is worked through, she is in a position to decide if her religious beliefs support abstinence from premarital sex.

The form of the statement, aside from its content, is an example of another resistance-neutralizing strategy borrowed from hypnosis where it is used to facilitate induction and popularized in its application to psychotherapy by Bandler and Grinder (1979, pp. 79-86). The intervention is that of pacing the client by accepting or accommodating client-initiated statements and then adding to the client's formulation therapist-induced statements. By accepting the client's statements, it is thought that the client is more likely to accept the therapist's next lead. In the same manner, a hypnotist may offer the subject a number of truisms that are highly likely to be agreed upon by the subject and then suggest a phenomenon the hypnotist would like the subject to experience (e.g., "You're resting in your chair. You can feel its warmth on your back. And you can notice you are becoming sleepy.") The astute reader may recognize pacing as an appeal to the social interest category of influence described in Chapter 2. The more similar the therapist appears in a variety of ways to an uncertain individual within this novel relationship, the more likely the susceptible client will be to follow the lead of the therapist for additional behavior.

In summary, resistance is a two-sided coin that is heavily

dependent upon whether one observes from the client's or the
therapist's point of view. From the vantage point of this chapter,
what is frequently labeled as resistance is largely a by-product of
conceptualization of what is possible or acceptable by *either* the
therapist or client that limits the range of responses and the
freedom with which alternatives are chosen. What Kuhn discovered in the flow of scientific advancement appears to be par-
alleled in individual advancement in psychotherapy: what
interferes with innovation is the significant impact of existing
solutions on conceptual thinking (see also Adams, 1974, pp.
70-71). As in the case of Mr. Caldwell, some limited changes can
be elicited by exploiting the rigidity of a particular model of the
world without actually modifying the model. A more elegant
outcome is one that goes beyond resistance in order to transform the model of the world itself. It is to methods geared to
prevent resistance, neutralize it, or even transform resistance
into motivation for second-order change that attention is now
directed.

REVISING WORLD MODELS AND DYSFUNCTIONAL BEHAVIORAL STRATEGIES

Sheldon Kopp (1973) has likened psychotherapy to a pil-
grimage toward personal growth. Unlike some pilgrimages that
begin with joy, therapy more frequently begins with fear and
tentativeness on the part of the pilgrims. He recommends therapists sidestep attempts on the part of the client to pull the therapist into the fantasy of taking care of the individual instead of
the client coming to care for himself. When the client falls to the
floor, he is puzzled and disappointed. But the client also has an
opportunity to get up and try something new. Much of therapy
appears to have this quality of producing the unfamiliar and unexpected within a relatively safe environment, of "bein' where
they ain't" so the client can do something different. By doing
something different, the client can become more of who he potentially is. Unfamiliarity is disorienting and unsettling, and it is
precisely from the frustration experienced within this disorientation that growth occurs. When expectancies are not met, the

conceptual underpinnings become soft and unsupportive. One's model of the world can undergo a second-order change because the familiar model is no longer predictive. If the relationship with the therapist is the expected one within the client's model of the world, no second-order change is likely to occur. Why should it? The current model of the world can accommodate the therapist's actions successfully.

Beginning artists learn the importance of making the familiar unfamiliar so that they can actually see what is there rather than attempt to draw what they think they see (Edwards, 1979, ch. 4). You can deomonstrate this phenomenon to yourself without having to be artistically inclined. Take any line drawing (a panel from a newspaper comic strip will do) and draw it right side up. Unless you are a trained artist, your product is unlikely to match well the stimulus picture. Now turn the picture upside down so that you can see it as an unfamiliar form, a series of lines and shapes connected one to the other. Beginning at the top of the inverted figure, study each line, moving from one line to the next until they are all connected together like a jigsaw puzzle. All that you need to know is before you in the lines. To interpret the lines or turn them right side up in your mind only complicates the task. Please resist this temptation. Instead, draw only the lines and shapes as they are presented. Most individuals discover their upside down picture to be far superior to the right side up version even though both are a picture of the same thing and they are far more familiar with the right side up rendering.

Lasting conceptual change for the client begins by leaving the familiar. To do so gives the client the opportunity to reinterpret experiences more realistically instead of simply accommodating new input to conform to preconceptions. Additionally, the uncertainty may heighten the effectiveness of therapeutic interventions infused with factors of influence. For these reasons, the therapeutic task is to provide an unusual yet constructive relationship that undermines resistance by rendering the familiar client model of the world dysfunctional or inoperative. This task can be accomplished by the therapist operating as an anomaly within the client's current conceptualization of the world. Repeated exposure to a therapist acting in this manner increases the probability that a given client's model will undergo a transformation into one that is more productive. The discussion in this chapter will be limited to less traditional therapeutic approaches that are more likely to be unexpected than are traditional intervention strategies for resistance. In fact, some readers may wish to consider using these strategies only after more conventional ones have not proven productive. The issue remains one of how a therapist can alienate a client from his current model of the world in a way that minimizes resistance to change. Let us review three broad categories of unusual responses that are designed to achieve this end.

Tactics of Benign Reframing

Reframing of symptoms is a redefinition of a set of circumstances so that the same facts are accounted for equally well, but take on a different meaning (see Watzlawick et al., 1974, p. 95 for an elaborated discussion). To describe the yellow fluid, mentioned earlier, as lemonade-colored or urine-colored equally accounts for the yellowness and fluidity of the liquid, but with widely disparate meanings attached. This interpretation, in turn, influences the way the individual will behave toward the fluid. When a therapist helps a client to reframe past history or present experience, he may similarly influence the client to react differently to similar circumstances in the future.

A therapist can usually assume that the way a client views his experience is not working well enough in that the best strategies derived from that conceptualization have been ineffective at resolving it. Therefore, by introducing a fresh definition of problems, the therapist provides an alternative perspective that may prove to be a stepping-stone to alternative ways of behaving. Unless done strategically, a therapist-introduced reframing that results in the client feeling blamed or criticized will likely only intensify resistance rather than dissolve it. For this reason, it is usually far more effective to separate intention from outcome. Specifically, a successful reframing usually takes the form of identifying a benign intention acceptable to the client and associating it with an undesirable behavioral outcome. The therapist and client can ally with the motive(s) and disengage from the means to satisfy the motive.

An example can bring these concepts to life. An ex-military officer began his therapy in a highly distressed state. His wife had threatened to leave him, his partner demanded he leave the professional corporation, and he was friendless. His approach to the therapy relationship gave ample evidence of how he arranged for his alienation. He behaved abruptly and belittlingly to the appointment secretary. Occasionally he would arrange an appointment, cancel it on short notice, and react angrily when another time was not available. He demanded that the therapist give up his evenings to see him so he would not have to rearrange his business day. Refusal was interpreted as betrayal. He made frequent phone calls to.the therapist and occasionally placed him on hold while he attended to another matter. Apologies were offered when they were self-serving and did not change the frequency of calls or holds. Limits were accepted begrudgingly. Requests were proffered as commands. While ostensibly in therapy to increase his awareness of how he put others off, most of his time was spent defending his actions and inferring malevolent motives on the part of others for not agreeing with or serving him. Given his narcissism, his guardedness and defensiveness, and his brittle self-esteem, he was unlikely to accept a direct statement concerning his insensitivity to the interests of others as a contributor to his isolation. An alternative was to recast the motives for his actions in terms of investment in his career that were, unfortunately, received as abrasiveness or hostility.

At first, he and his therapist talked at length about his commitment to his profession, his high aspirations, and the desirability of these pursuits. Before relating this to the effects of his self-absorption upon others, another preliminary step was undertaken. The reframing could become more credible by first helping him to acknowledge his reactions to others who were similarly self-absorbed. As the city in which he resided has a four-lane perimeter freeway with a median in the center for turns, he was readily able to identify his consternation at drivers who crossed the median to turn in the other direction, but left their car's tail in the traffic lane rather than fully in the median. He was asked whether those drivers behaved in this way to hurt or annoy other drivers, or because they were simply so caught up in their own interests they were disregarding the effect of their actions upon others. He agreed that, while they were self-centered, they were not intentionally inconsiderate.

Similarly, he identified his annoyance with grocery shoppers who left their shopping carts behind them at check-out lines when others were in line and with others who took time to balance their checkbooks at the teller window after a transaction rather than give way to others who are waiting. In each case, he agreed that their unwitting self-absorption had an abrasive effect upon others. The client then was informed that the way he felt around others who were preoccupied with their pursuits was the way others felt toward him, that his engrossment in career pursuits was experienced by others as lapses in consideration. The reframing sidestepped his proclivity to defend against feedback and to misinterpret it as malicious by separating a benign intention from a destructive outcome. He accepted the feedback and his behavior changed. Application of this procedure with others of similar personality organization has confirmed its utility.

Perhaps psychoanalysis emphasizes client resistance because within its framework the client is frequently asked to accept a reframing that ascribes unacceptable or sinister motives on the part of the client to a behavioral act (the Oedipal or Electra complexes are prime examples). Behavioral therapy, on the other hand, does not necessarily require the resistance construct because proponents ask clients to understand their problems in living within a far more neutral context of predictable outcomes according to the laws of learning. (This is not meant to imply that clients do not resist interventions derived from behavioral therapy.) Most intervention strategies, including the schools of psychoanalysis and behavior therapy, typically do not hold the client accountable for the etiology of the problems in living, only for doing something about them. That is, a fundamental reframing for most psychotherapy strategies is one that helps a client translate a symptom from something that happens to a client (and thus is out of one's control) to something that a client makes happen, or at least influences. Once a client can "own" a symptom, he is in a position to do something about it, rather than either despair or rely upon someone else to do something for him.

The understanding of a symptom as a positive intention expressed negatively is not a new concept (e.g., Haley, 1963, p. 139)—just an effective one. Satir (1967), Minuchin and Fishman (1981), and Madanes (1984) all emphasize recasting the identified patient in a family system from a negative to a positive role within the family. The symptom carrier is thought to operate as a preserver of the family system, distract others from sources of pain, or otherwise attempt to enhance the family's functioning. The attribution by the therapist is disarming. A typical Madanes (1984, p. 4) paradigm, for example, identifies symptomatic behavior of a child as an attempt to help the parents. The parents react to the child's behavior by focusing on the child to help him overcome "the problem." The parents' attempt to help actually perpetuates the problem behavior, precisely because the child's helplessness unites the parents. The therapist-ascribed motivation for the identified patient's behavior recasts it from oppositional or deficient to helpful and, by doing so, sets the stage for parents to react differently to the individual.

Minuchin reframes the family's understanding of a problem that results in a family schism to one that emphasizes a shared responsibility. (For example, "You act dependent upon your wife. What does she do that keeps you this way?") The issue becomes a family one requiring cooperative effort to resolve. An underlying positive intention is suggested and related to negative outcomes. (For example, "You're a very caring family who don't want to hurt each other so you tell white lies. But the indirectness leads to depression.") With this reframing, helping others to change enhances the self and unites the family.

Few individuals enter therapy to discover something terrible about themselves, although many expect to discover something horrible enough to be worthy of the intensity of their discomfort. No doubt this contributes to a client's difficulty in accepting responsibility for problems in living. Many clients initially externalize locus of control of symptoms (e.g., "The devil made me do it") or delegate responsibility for their expression to the nervous system ("bad nerves"), their unconscious ("I can't help it"), or genetics ("I was born this way"). Progress toward symptom ameliorization appears to be strongly related to the twin therapist tasks of refraining from meeting this client attribution while also relating positively to the client (see Boltari and Rappaport, 1983). Positive attribution of intention is thought to be helpful to these ends.

To reinterpret expressions of resistance and symptoms as creative strategies to solve a predicament that, unfortunately, will not work well enough can be quite unexpected by the client and highly affirming as well. Resistance almost always can be understood as an expression of the positive striving for self-protection or autonomy. For example, lying can be complimented as an excellent way to reduce acute interpersonal anxiety; but it is one that artifactually increases distrust and leads to greater anxiety in the future. The very strategy to resolve a problem actually exacerbates it and prevents recovery. Dependency can be reframed as a valuing of security. The task then becomes a cooperative one between client and therapist to help the client reach the goal of security, but more effectively through coming to depend upon oneself.

Rebelliousness can be relabeled as a valuing of independence while also not being sufficiently prepared for it because the client settles for reacting against authority rather than engaging in true self-direction. The client and therapist can cooperate in achieving the goal of independence. Anger can be re-identified from a "bad" feeling to a strength, the expression of which backfires (e.g., "Anger makes others back off. In that sense, your anger is a way to strive toward independence, only the way you use it winds up getting you left out"). Weeks and L'Abate (1982, p. 108) have reported a number of striking examples of relabelings for symptoms that the interested reader is invited to review.

Occasionally, a positive intention requires reframing into another positive intention to allow for an alternative behavioral outcome. For example, for parents having difficulty separating from their growing children, caring can be redefined from doing for ones' children to allowing them opportunities for them to do for themselves.

Not uncommonly, a client may argue that a positive inten-

tion justifies a devious means. For example, lying may be defended as a means of minimizing pain in another as in the following therapeutic dialog:

Client: I lied to her about my dating someone else because it
would hurt her if I told her I had.

Therapist: I believe you don't want to intentionally hurt
anyone, including yourself.

Client: No, I don't want to hurt either.

Therapist: I don't want to hurt you. Is it okay if I lie to you?

Client: No!

Therapist: Why not?

Client: It's not fair. Well, not exactly unfair. I'm here to get
at things. I want the truth.

Therapist: Can you think of an example where I told you
the truth about something, something hard to take?

Client: Yeah, about me putting others off by wanting too
much from them.

Therapist: How'd you feel about me telling you?

Client: It's funny. I didn't like hearing it, but I'd rather
know than not know. I'm doing it less.

Therapist: With better results?

Client: With better results—by far.

Therapist: How did you feel about me telling you?

Client: I didn't like hearing it. [Pause] I knew it already.

Therapist: I don't want to hurt you and I told you the truth
about something you didn't want to hear. It worked out
pretty well. You respect me. We still see each other.

Client: Yeah, but she'd dump me.

Therapist: Possibly. You've lied before and it's worked out
okay?

Client: Yeah, I've dated a lot of women and not told them I
was seeing others.

Therapist: How is it they're not dating you now?

Client: I didn't say it lasted.

Therapist: You mean lying saved the date but cost you the
relationship?

Client: Possibly.

Therapist: How possibly?

Client: Likely.

Therapist: How likely?

Client: Very likely. Okay.

Therapist: Okay. Lying doesn't get you the outcome you want in the long run and you see someone lying to you as not beneficial. What else might be motivating you to mislead her in addition to sparing her feelings? What does it do for you?

Client: I'm selfish, getting what I want without thinking of her.

Therapist: Think of something positive about you that might be motivating you.

Client: I can't.

Therapist: How would you feel if she dumped you?

Client: I'd hurt like hell.

Therapist: It sounds like at least part of your motivation is to protect yourself from hurt. Sounds good.

Client: Yeah, only it's not going to work in the long run.

Therapist: Let's see what else you can do to insulate yourself from most of the hurt, but in a way that continues relationships rather than breaks them off.

In this example, the motivation for lying is reframed from a means of minimizing pain in others to a means of protecting oneself from loss—both positive attributions. The therapist goes on to help the client see that neither intention is actualized and alternative means may be more successful.

At other times, a positively valued intention that leads to a negative outcome can be strategically reframed negatively in order to traverse a behavioral impasse. For example, a highly rigid and dominating woman interpreted her intrusiveness into the lives of others as protecting their interests. In doing so, she successfully alienated herself from most of her family. Her estrangement provoked considerable depression, but she felt very uncomfortable relinquishing control over the lives of others. Her domination was reframed as her difficulty in letting others give to her or do for her. She was placed in the uncomfortable position of having to refrain from telling others what to do to demonstrate to the therapist that she was quite capable of letting others do for her as they saw fit, or to continue to dominate, but to do so without the cloak of protecting others' interests.

Similarly, hyper-responsibility can be redefined as arrogance and a devaluation of the capabilities of others. If the interpretation is accepted, the client is placed in the uncomfortable position of continuing an undesirable behavior but at the expense of defining oneself and others negatively. The implication to the client is that he values self and others too much to continue a negatively defined behavior.

To the extent that psychotherapy is a placebo, the reframing does not even have to be true to modify behavior, only agreed upon by therapist and client. Fish (1973) has argued that the treatment in any therapy is "the ritual of therapy itself, invested with faith and expectancy by both healer and sufferer." O'Connell (1983) also has concluded that "good psychotherapy is successful employment of placebo principles regardless of therapeutic framework." If the reframing facilitates a beneficial change in behavior, whether it was accurate or not beforehand, it becomes true after the fact.

For example, Cohen (1984) has successfully helped adult children of abusive parents refrain from abusing their children or disengage from abusive partners by redefining the issue as one of loyalty to one's parents. To continue the pattern of abuse or allow it to happen ot oneself in one's current family is defined as an acknowledgement that one's parents were behaving appropriately. Once the client accepts the benign intention of family loyalty, he or she can become more receptive to explore with the therapist the possibility that the client was beaten, not because there was something wrong with the client, but because there was something wrong with the abusive parent. The initial reframing of current abuse as a by-product of loyalty to one's parents may help reduce resistance enough to the receptive client to make a more realistic evaluation of the current abuse and then seek a more productive expression of family loyalty currently. Whether the current pattern of abuse is actually an expression of family loyalty becomes relatively inconsequential to the profoundly positive behavioral changes that follow from acceptance of the proposition.

One half of the formula for reframing is an appeal to a valuing of oneself; the other half addresses a devaluation of the problematic behavior. The client with the dating problem above accepted the self-protective intention of his lying, but also came to identify the act as a relationship destroyer rather than a means of extending the life of a relationship. By separating the act from the intention he was able to complete the transformation. After accepting an unfamiliar interpretation of intention, a familiar activity that led to negative outcomes became estranged and unacceptable.

Not infrequently, clients will interpret a self-defeating behavior positively. As long as clients view a targeted behavior as an act of courage or a virtue, modification is unlikely to occur. For example, a school yard bully who derives a sense of strength and power from his dominance of others can be told matter-of-factly that strong boys who like themselves do not pick on smaller ones; strong boys help them out. The introduction of a credible alternative point of view introduces uncertainty and pause for reflection. The original conceptualization of the activity is disturbed. Another example is that of stubborn refusal to change being justified by a client as an expression of willpower. If the activity is recast as an expression of fearfulness it is no longer heroic to resist.

Negative reframings of behavior appeal to a client's concern about how his actions will be interpreted by others. Therefore, they are quite effective when the symptomatic behavior appears to be an attempt to influence the way others see the client. For example, an all too common phenomenon is that of a teenage drinker who equates the frequency and quantity of consumption with maturity. The adolescent can be asked if he has ever seen a ten-year-old smoking. Invariably, the client has had this experience and has reacted to the smoker with disdain. With little nudging, the client typically elaborates on how the ten-year-old sees himself as grown up and tough, but is not viewed that way even by the adolescent. In fact, many adolescents accurately identify early smoking as a sign of insecurity or an attempt to win peer approval or a bucking of authority. When the truculent adolescent is informed that the way he sees the ten-year-old smoker is the way most adults and many adolescents see his own drinking, much of the incentive to drink for the impression of maturity is deflated. The adolescent can then focus on the issue of developing true maturity through responsibility, replacing insecurity with security while also avoiding possible addiction.

Another example involving a couple addresses both the tendency of a client to frame maladaptive behavior as a virtue and the interpretation of client behavior on the part of others. A couple bickered a great deal, yet the threat of separation was reacted to by each with considerable anxiety. A variety of evidence strongly suggested that Mary both wanted to be identified as individuating within the marriage while also wanting to continue to depend upon John. John, on the other hand, both wanted the security of continuous companionship with Mary while also verbally supporting her stated desire for greater independence.

The couple appeared to be colluding with one another to maintain a highly dependent relationship behaviorally while verbally identifying it as one allowing considerable autonomy for each partner. A great deal of the frustration of both John and Mary appeared to be a result of this discrepancy between their actual and idealized relationship. At one point during a couple therapy session, John identified the husband's role in the marriage as one of responsibility for the welfare of the wife. Mary did not react to this, apparently because John's defined role appealed to her desire for security through John's protection. At the same time, the role contradicted her stated desire for self-responsibility. The therapist sincerely and earnestly looked at Mary and asked John if he really saw his wife as so helpless and irresponsible that he needed to be responsible for her welfare. By making the covert contract overt, the couple was afforded an opportunity to bring the verbally defined and the behaviorally observed relationship into greater accord.

Another example of appealing to the impact of one's behavior upon others sidesteps the issue of intention altogether by appealing solely to the impression one's behavior has on others. For example, an adolescent female had a history of lying in and out of therapy, but reacted to challenges by others with staunch denial of lying or even the intention of misrepresentation. A therapeutic response was "Whether you're lying or not, you come across as a liar. If you come across to me this way, you likely do to others as well. Is this the way you want to be seen by others?" The client is held accountable for the impression she created in others; no time was spent pursuing the usually elusive issue of whether the client is actually lying. This format for intervention can prove beneficial for a wide range of "disowned" dysfunctional behavior ranging from seductiveness to ingratiation.

Creating an Unfamiliar Therapeutic Relationship

Unlike social relationships, the one between client and therapist involves a contract to help at least one of the participants change. In the typical case, the relationship specifies a behavioral goal or goals that, once achieved, signals the end of the relationship. These goals are frequently made explicit in the therapeutic contract in order to provide a focus for the work together. The agreed upon goal becomes a marker used by the therapist to redirect a client when he either strays toward fulfillment of the covert goal or avoids sensitive issues. The covert goal is one that maintains the client's current model of the world in favor of others making changes; the overt goal transforms it. Any response of the form, "How is this helping you to reach your goal?" can be used to redirect a client from other-oriented support to self-support. Resistance may be experienced in the relationship between therapist and client at times when the therapist does not conform to client expectations based upon the client's current model of the world even if the therapist's behavior is in accord with mutually agreed upon overt goals.

In this discussion of reframing, emphasis was placed on the belief that if the therapist views the client's problems in living as the client does, change is unlikely to occur. Reframing offers an alternative framework to account for the evidence of a client's experience. Within the relationship between client and therapist, if the therapist responds in a manner wholly consistent with the client's expectations, change is also unlikely to occur. As long as the therapist behaves in a predictable manner (from the client's point of view), the client's model of the world appears accurate. The task is to relate in a manner that both undermines a dysfunctional world model while also facilitating change.

Suppose a client provocatively threatens to break off therapy at a point where termination appears to be against the client's best interests. An expected response might be one that intends to persuade the client to remain in therapy. By doing so the therapist risks unintentionally rewarding the client's self-defeating strategy of soliciting caring by threatening to withdraw from a relationship. To the extent that the client engages others outside of therapy in a similar fashion, the therapist would not want to mislead the individual that the strategy has long-term efficacy. Asocial responses might take the form of "Is that really what you want to do?" or "What can you predict if you follow through with this plan? Can you settle for that?"

This is not to suggest that a therapist would be unwise to initially accommodate a client's dysfunctional style of relating. Appreciating the client's view of the world frequently decreases defensiveness and increases receptivity to alternative frameworks since the client has had the opportunity to have his understanding communicated to the therapist. This accommodation is a form of pacing that precedes leading the client elsewhere.

Therapists, being socialized human beings, will feel the tug to conform to the expectancies created out of the client's model of the world for a particular situation. For example, a client arrives late to a session and brushes it off with "Sorry I'm late." The almost automatic socialized response for most individuals is acceptance (although repetition may evoke annoyance). Not infrequently, conscious effort is required to stand outside the universe of socialized responses in order to process the interaction therapeutically: "You came to therapy because you said others see you as irresponsible and you said you wanted to do something about that. Arriving late is something others will see as irresponsibility. Do you want to do something about that?"

The paradox of being an effective therapist is that one must simultaneously be highly socialized and desocialized. The socialized part of the therapist recognizes the aberrant behavior, knows of more appropriate behavior, and "reads" the implicit social demands offered in client communication. In the example above, the therapist noted that lateness interferes with relating to others. The therapist also "read" the subtle cue to treat the lateness lightly, but chose to respond outside the conventional responses of either dismissing the behavior or chiding the client in order to disengage the client from usual means of dealing with predictable reactions to lateness.

The socialized part of the therapist is also the part that renders him vulnerable to client manipulation. In his excellent discussion of the communication process in psychotherapy, Ernst Beier (1966) assumes that an individual's manner of interacting is not merely to defend his vulnerability, but also to actively influence the receiver. More specifically, covert cues diverge from the manifest content of a message and serve to create sets in the receiver that constrict the response alternatives of the receiver to predictable ones which are either safe or rewarding for the sender. The indirect attempts to "engage" the receiver can be outside awareness for both the sender and receiver although the outcomes remain predictable and self-perpetuating. By constricting the responses of another through covert cues in ambiguously encoded messages, the sender "diminishes the self-correcting devices available to the individual" (p. 282).

The hidden or indirect cues described by Beier to create an emotional climate beneficial to the sender's unaware wishes can be understood as those elements in the interaction process that work toward maintaining the client's current model of the world. Returning to the example above, the client who arrives late to commitments has little incentive to change as long as lateness is treated as insignificant. If others should respond with annoyance, on the other hand, the client is still in a position to perpetuate the tardiness: "Why should I cooperate with people who are annoyed with me?" Both the client and the recipient may feel self-righteously piqued and have little understanding of what the other is irritated about. To the extent that the client enages the therapist in the typical manner and the therapist responds accordingly, the faulty or self-limiting model is perpetuated within therapy as well.

The socialized therapist who provides asocialized responses is often in the position of knowing he is going in the right direction because it "feels" awkward on the inside! In order to be therapeutic, the cloak of politeness inherent in socialized discourse is often laid aside (although not necessarily tact along with it). Politeness frequently shares with manipulation the quality of indirectness (as in "I'd rather not" rather than a straight "no" as a refusal to a request), but is not exploitive. In therapy, on the other hand, direct, honest communication is encouraged. The therapist may bring up subjects that evoke discomfort in the client, an activity infrequently performed in usual social discourse. Who has not experienced discomfort when informing a friend that his fly is open or her blouse unbuttoned even though one knows the other individual would prefer to know? Therapists are further desocialized in relationships with clients because the relationship is not reciprocal. The usual give-and-take is replaced with "detached concern." Clients tolerate unfamiliar responses from their therapists not just because they are offered in the context of a caring relationship, but also because the client wants to hear something different from input offered by conventional purveyors of help whether they be friends, family, ministers, or self-help books.

The mental unlocking ideas offered in Chapter 3 can be applied by the practitioner to generate a diversity of possible responses outside the realm of convention. The utility of these alternatives is contingent upon the particular context of the therapeutic interaction. The therapist may find it useful to gain from the client an appreciation of early relationships with authority, beginning with parents. Using this as one extreme, the therapist can ask how he could respond to structure a relationship at the other extreme. This may serve as a conceptual stepping stone to structure the relationship at the optimal point somewhere in between.

For example, if an overcontrolled client is the product of hypercritical parents, the therapist may consider the counter-expected relationship of unconditional acceptance. For a client whose impulsivity was fostered by overly indulgent parents, a highly contingent relationship can be considered, outcomes anticipated, and steps taken to develop a relationship to yield desired outcomes. Along similar lines, if a client treats therapy as extremely serious business, it may be useful to generate considerable playfulness and vice versa. Clients who present themselves as fragile can be considered for a structure which emphasizes the therapist's seeing them as tough enough to handle the stresses. Others who present as tough or impenetrable may benefit from acknowledgement by the therapist of their softer sides underneath their protective crust. To abrasive, alienating clients, one can consider the beneficial effects of responding with greater closeness rather than backing away.

In short, extremes in client behavior can be counterposed by the therapist within the tolerance of the client to defamiliarize the client from his conceptual map of expected responses. The unfamiliar responses of the therapist are thought to have an unsettling effect upon the client's current model of the world. Beier (1966, pp. 55-66) describes the unsettling effect of asocial responses upon clients by therapists as "beneficial uncertainty."

> We propose that with the proper, disengaged response by a therapist, the patient is placed in a position where he can make more adequate choices. The therapist is not representing rational behavior to the patient, but rather a unique relationship which permits him to accept his transitory state of uncertainty without having to defend himself (p. 55).

According to Beier, for uncertainty to become beneficial it must occur in the context of a relationship that is not only asocial, but also one that minimizes judgment or hostility. Uncertainty aroused in a negative or hostile atmosphere is more likely to result in withdrawal or constricted responses.

It is thought that provocation of uncertainty is most productive within the confines of a relationship in which the client feels cared about. Unexpectedness can be pressed into the service of establishing and maintaining this caring relationship as well. In some form, clients expect their therapists to listen, to be kindly and attentive, and to encourage change within a 50-minute hour. For that reason, caring can be conveyed by performing unexpected actions that the therapist does not have to do. It might be asking an unassertive individual to join the therapist in a store in order to observe the therapist dealing assertively with salespeople. It might be holding the weekly therapy session with a socially withdrawn client at a series of local restaurants to promote desensitization. It might even take the form of varying traditional lengths of sessions and intervals between sessions.

Take a few minutes to review your caseload. Think of unexpected caring behavior you could offer to your clients. For now, deemphasize the impracticality of any of them in order to generate a number of options. Refer back to the option-expanding techniques from Chapter 3 if you need to. Now sift through the options for each client you selected. What outcomes can you predict for your client if you implemented one or another of them? What else? Are they desirable ones? Can you weave selected options into the fabric of your therapy? Pick one option for each client with which you are willing to experiment and see what happens.

Beier recommends creating beneficial uncertainty through either general disengagement responses or a variety of specific disengagement responses. General ones are of the "Go on" and "Umhum" variety that are offered in the absence of real understanding of the client, but do not conform to social expectations. For example, a general disengaged response to a provocative declaration of suicidal intent can take the form of "Tell me more" rather than the more socialized ones of "Please don't" or "That would be awful."

Among specific disengagement responses, Beier suggests interpretation, reflection of feelings, and probing. Each type of response steers clear of socialized responses of advice, support, reprimand, etc. in order to disorient the client from his conceptual model of the world and to reach a therapeutic objective. Applying these options to the tardy client generates a number of response alternatives:

"You appear bored with your therapy or angry with me." (Reflection of feeling)

"Are you late for others as well?" (Probing)

"Continuing to arrive late elsewhere will likely result in others being annoyed with you. Is this the way you want them to be?" (Interpretation)

Reframing has been described as a powerful means for developing an unfamiliar reconstruction of experience. The principle of reframing can be applied to the relationship between therapist and client as well. A return to the example of the self-centered ex-military officer from earlier in the chapter will demonstrate. The client expected a great deal of special treatment that was not only intrusive, but largely unnecessary. Minor upsets in his life were followed by "urgent" calls, demands for "emergency" appointments, and requests for minor tranquilization to ease the pain. Instead of conforming to the inappropriate demands, the therapist refused in a way that emphasized the therapeutic benefit of refusal. The client was informed that he was so fearful of pain that he had become phobic of it; therefore, to the extent that he stuck with the painful situation without rescue, the more able he would be to understand that pain, while uncomfortable, is not life-threatening. When he could eventually tolerate pain, he would not have to be so dependent upon others to relieve pain (an actual, albeit intolerable condition for him).

Similarly, by limiting calls to two per week, the therapist explained that he would fulfill his job by giving the client opportunities to develop confidence in himself and desensitize himself to pain while also not abandoning him. The therapist noted to the client that if pain were dulled artificially through medication, the client would have trouble keeping up motivation for treatment. The discomfort would serve as an incentive to develop skills to protect against future incidences. Because the client wanted supremacy over others, demands for excessive help from outside sources were defined as weakening. Therapist compliance with the excessive demands were reframed from fulfilling one's obligation to the client to sabotaging the client's progress. These interventions were accomplished within a relationship where the therapist had demonstrated in a number of ways his commitment to the client so that actions were far more likely to be interpreted as a rejection of his demands rather than of the client himself. For the same reason, they were unlikely to be thought of as merely a matter of therapist convenience.

A number of contemporary therapies have exploited the power of contra-expected or desocialized responses in the relationship between therapist and client. Of all of these, perhaps none has made disconfirming the client's expectations for the therapist's role as pivotal or extreme as Frank Farrelly's (Farrelly & Brandsma, 1974). Farrelly provokes the client into a number of experiences that leaves the client astonished, incredulous, uncertain, and even (at times) outraged. Yet boredom or disinterest is not reported and the healthy return rate after an initial interview of 95 percent (p. 132) supports the efficacy of his approach in qualified hands with receptive clients.

The strategy is almost to reverse the expected therapist role by having the therapist side with and become the negative half of the client's ambivalence toward self, others, and life's goals and values (p. 57). By joining the client's resistance and urging the client to continue the status quo, the client is frequently provoked to adopt an opposing view and more adaptive coping behavior. Farrelly assumes the client has not as yet made necessary changes because the client will not and, far from being fragile, can change if he so chooses (pp. 37-42). His burlesque of the client's resistance to change is done with a great deal of humor, parody, and sense of the absurd so that it is rarely misunderstood.

Client feedback has been reported to be highly positive. One client aptly summarized client reactions to Farrelly as the ". . . kindest, most understanding, warmly accepting person I've ever met in my whole life, wrapped up in the biggest son-of-a-bitch I've ever met" (pp. 132-135). When applied effectively, Farrelly has reported initial surprise on the part of the client followed by a reorganization of "expectational systems" toward the therapist, the culmination of which is client mobilization of adaptive behavior to counteract the therapist's skewed definition of the client. Once gains are consolidated and integrated, the characterizations adopted by the therapist are "out of date" and dropped (pp. 129-142).

Farrelly has found that by justifying to a client why he should remain as he is, the client becomes more invested in change. Resistance is low because no modification is imposed from the outside. More moderate implementation of this principle of sanctioning a client's symptomatic behavior and even encouraging resistance to change has enjoyed considerable popularity in psychotherapy systems that employ paradoxical intention (to be discussed in next section). Suggesting that a resistant client continue an undesirable behavior within the therapeutic relationship compels him to abandon the behavior in order to resist the therapist.

A variation of siding with the resistance is borrowed from hypnosis. When a suggestion is followed by anything but the suggested response, a hypnotist will define whatever occurs as either better than the requested response or a sign of deepening hypnosis. Regardless of what the subject does, the behavior is defined as cooperation. For example, at an initial session a client revealed her conflict about seeking therapy without having informed her husband. Because changes in her would impact upon the marriage she felt obligated to inform him, but also feared his reaction. The therapist believed the expected response was for him to attempt to persuade her to tell her spouse even though she was unwilling at the present time. Instead, she was asked if she would be willing not to tell him that day. It was thought that posing the dilemma was a means on her part to test whether the therapist would attempt to compel her to do things she did not want to do or did not feel strong enough to do. By accommodating her early resistance, she felt relief, went on to disclose a number of relevant intimacies, and told her husband anyway.

Another option of the therapist in relation to clients is to assume the "one down" position. If the therapist presents himself as already defeated, the client cannot easily further derogate the therapist by resisting; thus, there is little incentive to be oppositional. For example, a client judged to be intentionally noncommunicative can have requests for information presented with "You're probably going to say 'I don't know' to this and there's nothing I can do about it; but I request you think about it before answering." Providing the "I don't know" response in this context actually affirms the therapist's credibility.

Another example involves a highly sensitive, constricted, and shy young woman who came to therapy because social isolation had become painfully depressing. Her only social outlet was church membership. Her bland clothing was matched by her deficient spontaneity, and her excessive guilt-proneness punctuated her timidity. While regularly attending therapy for close to a year and becoming less depressed, she continued to struggle with engaging others, dating men, and risking herself for promotional opportunities for which she was qualified. Eventually she decided to return to Ohio. She used her last session to express her gratitude for her therapy.

Rather than thank her or review her progress as anticipated, the therapist opted to tap her guilt-proneness in her behalf. He lamented that although he had tried his best, he had not been able to help her to engage others more successfully and that he regretted letting her down. She pointed out to him her higher opinion of herself and all the positive changes she had made. She vowed to continue to improve in the future. She continued to write each year at Christmas for years after. Each time she brought her therapist up to date on her job advancements and her success at loving relationships. Her guilty self-effacement had been replaced by accomplishment and satisfaction.

Unusual Behavioral Prescriptions

In addition to using the relationship between therapist and client to disintegrate faulty client conceptualization that leads to resistance, the therapist may also promote more effective reintegration by requesting that the client perform unusual and strategic behavioral assignments. To stimulate second-order change, the assignment must be one that cannot be assimilated into or accounted for by the client's current framework. That is, the assignment appears paradoxical from the point of view of the client's model of the world.

Riebel (1984) has provided a well organized and highly readable review of paradoxical rationales to overcome resistance, disturb systems, and alter client perspectives. She defines paradoxical intervention strategies as those which "send two messages on different levels, one of which both qualifies and contradicts the other." The most typical format for a paradoxical intervention is to instruct the client to voluntarily produce or even extend the symptomatic behavior which the client has sought help to alleviate. Unlike pathological double binds in which the client cannot win, with this therapeutic double bind he cannot lose. If the client resists, he does so by reducing the target behavior. If he continues or intensifies the symptomatic behavior then the behavior is redefined as a voluntary rather than an involuntary act. When the behavior is something the client does rather than something that happens to the client, the client is placed in the uncompromising position of being held responsible for regulating the symptom.

The double-binding strategies can be used to introduce self-enhancing behavioral assignments to resistant clients. For example, if a therapist says, "I've got something in mind for you that you're not going to want to do . . ." or "You may see this as too difficult for you to do . . ." the client has the option of either proving the therapist wrong by cooperating or validating the therapist by declining the assignment.

Haley (1963, pp. 25-26) reported Milton Erickson's ingenious solution to the problem of getting a client to follow directives while also autonomously making decisions. Erickson would ask a client to choose between two directives, the one he would like the client to choose to perform or an alternative one that would be more difficult or unpleasant. Invariably, the client would choose the less noxious alternative. This "worse alternative" approach corresponds to a variant of the reciprocation principle of social influence that may be labeled "reciprocal concession." Indebtedness can be evoked not just in response to an initial favor, but also in response to an initial concession. The therapist presents a more noxious request as the desired assignment, but "settles for" the alternative. The client is put in the position of reciprocating by agreeing to at least perform the less noxious, but still beneficial, assignment.

Haley has raised a similar strategy to its ultimate refinement to date in his innovation of ordeal therapy (Haley, 1984). The premise is simple: if one makes it more difficult for a person to have a symptom than to give it up, the person will give up the symptom. After the problem is clearly defined, the therapist solicits a commitment from the client to overcome the problem. The therapist informs the client that an effective means to end the symptom is available, but it may be difficult. Before the ordeal is described, the client is further informed that the means is within the client's capabilities and will not violate the client's morality. A commitment to carry through the ordeal is typically sought before it is negotiated with the client. The ordeal itself is something that is both severe and good for the client (exercise, study, etc.). The ordeal is given a rationale and is to be continued until the problem is resolved. The properly selected ordeal may have ramifications for all in the client's social context.

By way of example, consider the case cited by Haley of a teenager who would insert a number of household items in his anus. His stepmother was left to clean the bathroom of leftover material. The therapist recognized that the stepmother was being burdened with the consequences of the problem while the father was not. In part, the symptom was also thought to function as a means to distract the parents from their marital problems. An ordeal was designed to not only make the symptom burdensome for the identified client, but also to place responsibility for its resolution in the hands of the father. Each evening after the boy placed items in his anus, the father was to take him into the backyard and supervise the digging of a 3 × 3 × 3 foot hole within which the material was to be buried. This ordeal was to be repeated on each occasion for as long as the symptom occurred. Before long the boy lost enthusiasm for the symptom. The father, pleased with his success with his boy, associated more with him. The wife, pleased with her husband's success, became closer to him.

The subtlety of this ordeal deserves closer examination. On one level it is a beneficial ordeal for the son through exercise. On another level, sitting in the cold with his son until the hole was completed was a greater ordeal for the father than taking responsibility for his share of the parenting. On still another level, the ordeal was a metaphorical use of paradoxical intent. Since the son was already putting things in a hole, the therapist asked him to continue placing the material in a hole, one that was bigger and deeper.

This ordeal and other well-constructed ones similar to it have an affinity to factors potentiating the principle of influence described earlier as commitment and consistency. Commitments that are declared publicly, require effortful action, and compel personal responsibility for actions performed are also those most likely to result in modifications in beliefs so that the beliefs become more consistent with the committed behavior. The therapeutic ordeal is an activity the commitment to which is declared openly to the therapist. An ordeal by definition is certainly effortful. The client agrees beforehand to perform the ordeal, thus relieving the therapist of responsibility for "forcing" the client to perform. Furthermore, because the activity is not satisfying, participation cannot be justified on the basis of rewarding consequences inherent in the activity. The ordeal may be effective in changing a client's relationship to his symptom, not only because it is not rewarding, but also because the client must accept responsibility for choosing to perform an activity more distressing than the symptom itself. Apparently, the factors that contribute to modifying beliefs to be in accord with one's behavior may also contribute to modifying beliefs that maintain a symptom if the occurrence of the symptom serves as a cue to perform a self-induced aversive activity.

Weeks and L'Abate (1982) have completed the difficult task of compiling a catalog of a variety of paradoxical methods extending all the way from forbidding changes in order to facilitate them even to prescribing relapses! The interested reader will find this to be a rich source of unusual intervention strategies.

Resistance can serve both to identify the conceptual impasse for either client or therapist and to be the raw material of a more efficient conceptual framework from which to proceed behaviorally. The transformation may appear unusual: "Absurd dilemmas require absurd solutions" (Haley, 1984, p. 4). After all, what becomes of the prince who hops like a frog if the princess asks him to go right on hopping, but to do so slowly, one leg at a time?

The Value of "Not Doing"

Another option of the therapist to facilitate self-discovery is to become like the pause in the beats of music: not to interfere, not to do too much, not to work too hard. Once the process of change is undertaken, silence can be an expression of faith in the other person's potential to become more of himself.

So, I'll be quiet now.

REFERENCES

Adams, J. L. *Conceptual blockbusting: A guide to better ideas.* San Francisco: W. H. Freeman & Co., 1974.

Albrecht, K. *Brain power: Learn to improve your thinking skills.* Englewood Cliffs, N.J.: Prentice-Hall, 1980.

Arieti, S. *Creativity: The magic synthesis.* New York: Basic Books, 1976.

Bandler, R. Hypnosis as an Application of Neurolinguistic Programming. Workshop given in Atlanta, October 1980.

Bandler, R., & Grinder, J. *The structure of magic* (Vol. 1). Palo Alto, CA: Science and Behavior Books, 1975.

Bandler, R., & Grinder, J. *Frogs into princes.* Moab, Utah: Real People Press, 1979.

Bandler, R., Grinder, J., & Satir, V. *Changing with families.* Palo Alto, CA.. Science and Behavior Books, 1976.

Bandura, A. Behavioral modification through modeling procedures. In L. Krasner & L. P. Ullmann (Eds.), *Research in behavior modification.* New York: Holt, Rinehart, & Winston, 1966.

Beck, A. T., Rush, A. J., Shaw, B. F., & Emery, G. *Cognitive therapy for depression.* New York: Guilford Press, 1979.

Beier, E. G. *The silent language of psychotherapy.* New York: Aldine, 1966.

Berlitz, C. *Native tongues.* New York: Grosset & Dunlap, 1982.

Berne, E. *Transactional analysis in psychotherapy.* New York: Grove Press, 1961.

Bertelson, P. The Nature of hemispheric specialization: Why should there be a single principle? *The Behavioral and Brain Sciences,* 1981, *4,* 63-64.

Boltari, M. A., & Rappaport, H. The relationship of patient and therapist-reported experiences of the initial session to outcome: An initial investigation. *Psychotherapy: Theory, Research, and Practice,* 1983, *20,* 355-358.

Brandell, J. R. Stories and storytelling in child psychotherapy. *Psychotherapy: Theory, Research, Practice, and Training,* 1984, *21,* 54-62.

Bruner, J. S. *On knowing: Essays for the left hand.* Cambridge: Harvard University Press, 1962.

Bruner, J. S., & Postman, L. On the perception of incongruity: A paradigm. *Journal of Personality,* 1949, *18,* 206-223.

Bugelski, B. R. *The psychology of learning applied to teaching* (rev. ed.). New York: Macmillan, 1964, 1971.

Buzan, T. *Use both sides of your brain.* New York: Dutton, 1976.

Cautela, J. R. Treatment of compulsive behavior by covert sensitization. *Psychological Record,* 1966, *16,* 33-41.

Cialdini, R. *Influence: How and why people agree to things.* New York: William Morrow & Co., 1984.

Cohen, P. Violence in the family—An act of loyalty. *Psychotherapy: Theory, Research, Practice, and Training,* 1984, *21,* 249-259.

Confer, W. N., & Ables, B. S. *Multiple personality: Etiology, diagnosis, and treatment.* New York: Human Sciences Press, 1983.

Craik, F. I. M., & Lockhart, R. S. Levels of processing. *Journal of Verbal Learning,* 1972, *11,* 671-684.

Deikman, A. Bimodal consciousness. *Archives of General Psychiatry,* 1971, *25,* 481-489.

Edwards, B. *Drawing on the right side of the brain.* Los Angeles: J. P. Tarcher, 1979.

Ellis, A., & Harper, R. *A new guide to rational living.* North Hollywood: Wilshire Book Co., 1975.

Farrelly, F., & Brandsma, J. *Provocative therapy.* San Francisco: Shields, 1974.

Festinger, L. *A theory of cognitive dissonance.* Evanston, IL: Row-Peterson, 1957.

Fish, J. *Placebo therapy.* San Francisco: Jossey-Bass, 1973.

Freedman, J. L., & Fraser, S. C. compliance without pressure: The foot-in-the-door technique. *Journal of Personality and Social Psychology,* 1966, *4,* 195-203.

Gardner, R. A. *Dr. Gardner's modern fairy tales.* Cresskill, NJ: Creative therapeutics, 1977.

Garfield, S. L., & Bergin, A. E. *Handbook of psychotherapy and behavioral change: An empirical analysis* (2nd. ed.). New York: John Wiley & Sons, 1978.

Gottman, J. M., & Leiblum, S. R. *How to do psychotherapy and how to evaluate it.* New York: Holt, Rinehart, & Winston, Inc., 1974.

Grinder, J., & Bandler, R. *Structure of magic* (Vol. 2). Palo Alto, CA: Science and Behavior Books, 1976.

Haley, J. *Strategies of psychotherapy.* New York: Grune & Stratton, 1963.

Haley, J. *Uncommon therapy.* New York: W. W. Norton, 1973.

Haley, J. *Problem-solving therapy.* San Francisco: Jossey-Bass, 1976.

Haley, J. *Ordeal therapy.* San Francisco: Jossey-Bass, 1984.

Hayakawa, S. I. *Language in thought and action* (3rd. ed.). New York: Harcourt, Brace, & Jovanovich, 1972.

Jaynes, J. *The origin of consciousness in the breakdown of the bicameral mind.* Boston: Houghton-Mifflin, 1976.

King, G., & Confer, W. N. Ethics: Is informed deceit the answer to informed consent? *Psychology Today,* May 1978, pp. 36-37.

Koestler, A. *The act of creation.* New York: MacMillian, 1964.

Kopp, S. B. *If you meet the Buddha on the road, kill him!* New York: Banton, 1973.

Kuhn, T. S. *The structure of scientific revolutions.* Chicago: University of Chicago Press, 1962.

Laughter, the best medicine. *Readers Digest,* November 1984, p. 141.

Lazare, A., & Eisenthal, S. Patient requests in a walk-in clinic. *Journal of Nervous and Mental Disease,* 1977, *165,* 330-340.

Madanes, C. *Behind the one-way mirror.* San Francisco: Jossey-Bass, 1984.

Maslow, A. H. *Toward a psychology of being* (2nd. ed.). New York: Van Nostrand Reinhold, 1968.

May, R. *Courage to create.* New York: Norton, 1975.

Milgram, S. Behavioral study of obedience. *Journal of Abnormal and Social Psychology,* 1963, *67,* 371-378.

Milgram, S. *Obedience to authority.* New York: Harper & Row, 1974.

Miller, G. A. The magical number seven, plus or minus two: Some limits on our capacity for processing information. *Psychological Review*, 1956, *63*, 81-97.

Minuchin, S., & Fishman, H. S. *Family therapy techniques.* Cambridge: Harvard University Press, 1981.

Mosak, H. H., & Dreikurs, R. Adlerian psychotherapy. In R. Corsini (Ed.), *Current psychotherapies.* Itasca, IL: F. E. Peacock Publications, 1973.

Naisbett, J. *Megatrends.* New York: Warner Books, 1982.

Nebes, R. D. Direct examination of cognitive function in the right and left hemispheres. In M. Kinsbourne (Ed.), *Asymetrical functions of the brain.* New York: Cambridge University Press, 1978.

O'Connell, S. The placebo effect and psychotherapy. *Psychotherapy: Theory. Research, and Practice*, 1983, *20*, 337-345.

Palazzoli, M. S., Boscolo, L., Cecchin, G. F., & Prata, G. Family rituals: A powerful tool in family therapy. *Family Process*, 1977, *16*, 445-454.

Parnes, S. J. *Creative behavior workbook.* New York: Charles Scribner's Sons, 1967.

Perls, F. *Gestalt therapy verbatim.* Moab, Utah: Real People Press, 1969.

Prochaska, J. *Systems of psychotherapy: A transtheoretical analysis.* Homewood, IL: Dorsey Press, 1979.

Prochaska, J., & DiClemente, C. C. Transtheoretical therapy: Toward a more integrative model of change. *Psychotherapy: Theory, Research, and Practice*, 1982, *19*, 276-288.

Rabkin, R. *Strategic psychotherapy.* New York: Basic Books, 1977.

Regan, D. T. Effects of a favor and liking on compliance. *Journal of Experimental Social Psychology*, 1971, 7, 627-639.

Rice, L. N. Therapist's style of participation and case outcome. *Journal of Consulting Psychology*, 1965, *29*, 155-160.

Rico, G. L. *Writing the natural way.* Los Angeles: J. P. Tarcher, 1983.

Riebel, L. Paradoxical intention strategies.. A review of rationales. *Psychotherapy: Theory, Research, Practice, and Training*, 1984, *21*, 260-272.

Rosen, S. (Ed.). *My voice will go with you: The teaching tales of Milton Erickson, M.D.* New York: Norton, 1982.

Rudestam, K. E. Semantics and psychotherapy. *Psychotherapy: Theory, Research, and Practice*, 1978, *15*, 190-192.

Rush, A. J., & Giles, D. E. Cognitive therapy: Theory and research. In

A. J. Rush (Ed.), *Short-term psychotherapies for depression.* New York: Guilford Press, 1982.

Satir, V. *Conjoint family therapy* (rev. ed.). Palo Alto, CA: Science and Behavior Books, 1967.

Satir, V. *Peoplemaking.* Palo Alto, CA: Science and Behavior Books, 1972.

Sherman, M. H. Siding with the resistance versus interpretation: Role implications. In M. C. Nelson, B. Nelson, M. H. Sherman, & H. S. Stream (Eds.), *Roles and paradigms in psychotherapy.* New York: Grune & Stratton, 1980.

Tolman, E. C. Principles of purposeful behavior. In S. Koch (Ed.), *Psychology: A study of science* (Vol. 2). New York. McGraw-Hill, 1959.

van der Hart, O. *Rituals in psychotherapy: Transition and continuity.* New York: Irvington, 1983.

van der Hart, O., & Ebbers, J. Rites of separation in Strategic Psychotherapy. *Psychotherapy: Theory, Research, and Practice,* 1981, *18*, 188-194.

von Oech, R. *A whack on the side of the head.* New York: Warner Books, 1983.

Wachtel, P. What should we say to our patients? On the wording of therapists' comments. *Psychotherapy: Theory, Research, and Practice,* 1980, *17*, 183-188.

Watzlawick, P. *The language of change.* New York: Basic Books, 1978.

Watzlawick, P., Weakland, J. H., & Fisch, R. *Change: Principles of problem formation and problem resolution.* New York: W. W. Norton & Co., 1974.

Weeks, G. Toward a dialectical approach to intervention. *Human Development,* 1977, *20*, 277-292.

Weeks, G., & L'Abate, L. *Paradoxical psychotherapy.* New York: Brunner/Mazel, 1982?

Whitaker, C. The symptomatic adolescent—An AWOL family member. In M. Sugar (Ed.), *The adolescent in group and family therapy.* New York: Brunner/Mazel, 1975.

Wolpe, J. *Psychotherapy by reciprocal inhibition.* Palo Alto, CA: Stanford University Press, 1958.

Worchel, S., Lee, J., & Adewole, A. Effects of supply and demand on ratings of object value. *Journal of Personality and Social Psychology,* 1975, *32*, 906-914.

Wright, S. A little less magic, please. *Family Therapy Networker*, 1985, *9*, 26-29.

Wyke, M. A. The nature of cerebral hemispheric specialization in man: Quantitative vs. qualitative differences. *The Behavioral and Brain Sciences*, 1981, *4*, 78-79.

Yalom, I. *Existential psychotherapy*. New York: Basic Books, 1980.

Zeig, J. K. (Ed.). *Ericksonian approaches to hypnosis and psychotherapy*. New York: Brunner/Mazel, 1982.

Zeigarnik, B. Über das bebalten von erledigten und unerledigten. *Psychologia Forsch*, 1927, *9*, 1-85. (Also in N. L. Munn, L. D. Fernald, & P. S. Fernald. *Basic Psychology* (3rd. ed.). Boston: Houghton-Mifflin, 1972.)

NAME INDEX

181

SUBJECT INDEX

An Invitation

Genius . . . means little more than the faculty of perceiving in an unhabitual way.

—William James

Interested readers are invited to send examples of innovative metaphors and unusual, but effective, interventions of all types for possible inclusion in a future compilation. When specific case material is cited, written client authorization for disclosure in a professional publication is necessary. Correspondence may be addressed to:

W. N. Confer, Ph.D.
Clinical Director
Wiregrass Comprehensive Mental Health System
P. O. Drawer 1245
Dothan, AL 36302